# Gilded Age
# and Progressive Era

*Reference Library
Cumulative Index*

# Gilded Age and Progressive Era

*Reference Library*
*Cumulative Index*

## CUMULATES INDEXES FOR:

*Gilded Age and Progressive Era: Almanac*

*Gilded Age and Progressive Era: Biographies*

*Gilded Age and Progressive Era: Primary Sources*

*Lawrence W. Baker, Project Editor*

**U·X·L**
*An imprint of Thomson Gale,*
*a part of The Thomson Corporation*

**THOMSON**
**GALE**

Detroit • New York • San Francisco • New Haven, Conn. • Waterville, Maine • London

# THOMSON
## ✦
### GALE

## Gilded Age and Progressive Era Reference Library Cumulative Index

**Project Editor**
Lawrence W. Baker

**Rights and Acquisitions**
Margaret Abendroth, Emma Hull,
Jackie Jones, Jacqueline Key, Andrew Specht

**Imaging and Multimedia**
Dean Dauphinais, Lezlie Light,
Michael Logusz

**Product Design**
Pamela Galbreath, Jennifer Wahi

**Composition**
Evi Seoud

**Manufacturing**
Rita Wimberley

**LIBRARY OF CONGRESS CATALOGING-IN-PUBLICATION DATA**

Gilded Age and Progressive Era reference library cumulative index / Lawrence W. Baker,
index coordinator.
    p. cm.
    ISBN-13: 978-1-4144-0197-3 (softcover : alk. paper) --
    ISBN-10: 1-4144-0197-3 (softcover : alk. paper) --
    1. Valentine, Rebecca. Gilded Age and Progressive Era -- Indexes. 2. United States --
History -- 1865–1921 -- Juvenile literature -- Indexes. 3. United States -- History -- 1865–1921 --
Biography -- Juvenile literature -- Indexes. 4. United States -- History -- 1865–1921 --
Sources -- Juvenile literature -- Indexes. 5. Almanacs, American -- Juvenile literature --
Indexes.
I. Baker, Lawrence W.
    E661.V35 2006
    973.803 -- dc22
                                                                              2006023052

This title is also available as an e-book.
ISBN-13: 978-1-4144-1046-3, ISBN-10: 1-4144-1046-8
Contact your Thomson Gale sales representative for ordering information.
Printed in the United States of America
10 9 8 7 6 5 4 3 2 1

# Gilded Age and Progressive Era Reference Library Cumulative Index

**Bold italic** type indicates set titles. **Bold** type indicates main *Biographies* entries and their page numbers. Illustrations are marked by (ill.).

*A = Gilded Age and Progressive Era: Almanac; B = Gilded Age and Progressive Era: Biographies; PS = Gilded Age and Progressive Era: Primary Sources*

## A

AA (Alcoholics Anonymous)
    *B:* 250
AAAS (American Association for the Advancement of Science)
    *PS:* 139
Abolition movement
    *B:* 204
Accommodationism
    *PS:* 99, 100
Act for the Preservation of American Antiquities of 1906. *See* American Antiquities Act of 1906
Adams, Lewis
    *B:* 230
Adamson Act of 1916
    *A:* 278
**Addams, Jane**
    *A:* 187, 187 (ill.)
    *B:* 1 (ill.), **1–9**
    early years, *B:* 2
    feminism, *B:* 7
    Hull-House, *B:* 1, 3–7
    pacifism, *B:* 8
    Solomon, Hannah, *B:* 193
    Wells-Barnett, Ida B., *B:* 242
Addams, John
    *B:* 2

*The Adventures of Huckleberry Finn* (Twain)
    *A:* 210
    *B:* 212, 215
*The Adventures of Tom Sawyer* (Twain)
    *B:* 212, 215
Advertising
    *A:* 23, 116, 202, 204–5
    *PS:* 177
Aeronautics
    *A:* 244–47
AFL (American Federation of Labor)
    *A:* 53–54, 57
African Americans
    agriculture, *A:* 132
    boxing, *A:* 222
    civil rights movement, *B:* 233–34, 242
    Cleveland, Grover, *A:* 157; *B:* 20
    Columbian Exposition, *A:* 203; *PS:* 85–94
    convict lease system, *PS:* 87, 88
    education, *A:* 195; *B:* 233–34
    eugenics, *A:* 176
    Jim Crow laws, *A:* 138–39
    labor movement, *A:* 141
    lynching, *A:* 140–41; *B:* 128, 237, 239, 240 (ill.), 241–42, 243

McKinley, William, *A:* 165; *B:* 128
    northern migration, *A:* 94–95, 275
    political party affiliation, *A:* 6
    populism, *A:* 141–42
    during Reconstruction Era, *A:* 1–3
    reform movements, *A:* 180
    Roosevelt, Theodore, *A:* 262, 269; *B:* 159
    segregation, *B:* 238, 239; *PS:* 97–103
    soldiers, *A:* 101
    on *Titanic, PS:* 225
    Tuskegee Institute, *B:* 229, 230–32
    voting rights, *PS:* 74, 97, 98
    women, *PS:* 80–81
    women's suffrage, *B:* 207; *PS:* 77
Agricultural laborers
    *PS:* 126
Agriculture
    costs, *A:* 128
    economic depression, *A:* 130–33
    economy, *A:* 1, 21
    famine, *A:* 73
    Native American, *A:* 103

political aspects, *A:* 8–9, 133–36, 134 (ill.)
sustainable, *A:* 120–21
Agriculture, U.S. Department of
  *A:* 123, 124
  *B:* 164
  *PS:* 172
AIA (Archeological Institute of America)
  *PS:* 139
Aircraft
  *A:* 245–47, 246 (ill.)
Alaska
  *A:* 233–37, 239–41
  *B:* 77–79, 135
Alaska Game Act of 1902
  *PS:* 48
Alcohol abstinence.
  *See* Temperance movement
Alcohol moderation movement.
  *See* Temperance movement
Alcohol, movement against.
  *See* Temperance movement
Alcoholics Anonymous (AA)
  *B:* 250
Alcoholism
  *B:* 250
Aldrich, Nelson
  *A:* 272
Alexander, Freddie
  *B:* 108
Ali, Omar H.
  *A:* 142
Almshouses
  *A:* 196
Alpha Suffrage Club of Chicago
  *B:* 242–43
Altgeld, John
  *A:* 57
Amalgamated Association of Iron, Steel and Tin Workers
  *A:* 54–56
  *B:* 57
Amalgamated Clothing Workers of America
  *B:* 200

American Antiquities Act of 1906
  *A:* 268
  *B:* 164
  *PS:* 139–49
  Carter, Jimmy, *PS:* 147
  Clinton, Bill, *PS:* 147
  Hewett, Edgar Lee, *PS:* 139–40, 142–44
  legacy of, *PS:* 147–48
  Roosevelt, Franklin D., *PS:* 147
  Roosevelt, Theodore, *PS:* 48, 145–46
  text of, *PS:* 144–45
American Association for the Advancement of Science (AAAS)
  *PS:* 139
American Civil War
  *B:* 143
American Eugenics Society
  *A:* 176
American Federation of Labor (AFL)
  *A:* 53–54, 57
American Frontier. *See also* American West
  *A:* 110–11, 112
American Horse (Native American warrior)
  *A:* 110
American Indians. *See* Native Americans
American Medical Association
  *A:* 175
*American Mosaic: The Immigrant Experience in the Words of Those Who Lived It*
  *PS:* 198
American Party
  *A:* 76
American Railway Union (ARU)
  *A:* 56, 57, 58
American South. *See* Southern states
American system. *See* Mass production
American Tobacco
  *B:* 163

American West. *See also* Westward expansion
  mythology of, *PS:* 41–42
  Remington, Frederic, *PS:* 44
  Roosevelt, Theodore, *PS:* 42–47
American Woman Suffrage Association (AWSA)
  *A:* 182
  *B:* 207
  *PS:* 74, 76
Anarchism
  *B:* 53, 55–56
Ancient Order of Hibernians (AOH)
  *A:* 42–43, 45–48
Angel Island
  *PS:* 1, 2 (ill.)
Annexation
  *A:* 165–67
  *B:* 90, 128–29
Anthony, Susan B.
  *A:* 182
  *PS:* 74, 76, 80
  Gage, Matilda Joslyn, *B:* 208, 209
  Solomon, Hannah, *B:* 193, 198
  Stanton, Elizabeth Cady, *B:* 203, 206 (ill.), 206–8
Anthracite coal mining. *See* Coal mining
Anti-imperialism. *See also* Expansionism
  *A:* 165, 167, 265, 266, 278–79
  *B:* 128, 164, 216, 217
Anti-Imperialist League
  *A:* 266
Antiquities Act of 1906. *See* American Antiquities Act of 1906
Anti-Saloon League
  *B:* 248
Anti-Semitism. *See also* Pogroms
  *A:* 76, 82–86
  *B:* 54
  *PS:* 22–23, 24

Antitrust actions. *See also*
  Sherman Antitrust Act of 1890
    **B:** 86, 156–58, 163
    **PS:** 153, 158–59, 160
    Roosevelt, Theodore, **A:** 34,
      36–37, 260, 264–65
    Taft, William Howard, **A:** 272
    Wilson, Woodrow, **A:** 34–35,
      277, 278
Antiwar movement
  **A:** 266
  Addams, Jane, **B:** 8
  Goldman, Emma, **B:** 61–62
AOH (Ancient Order of
  Hibernians)
  **A:** 42–43, 45–48
Apache
  **B:** 188–89
*Appeal to Reason* (newspaper)
  **B:** 176
Arbor Day
  **A:** 121
Archeological Institute of America
  (AIA)
  **PS:** 139
Archeological sites
  **PS:** 139–40, 142–43, 147–48
Architecture
  **A:** 218
  **PS:** 178
Armed forces
  **B:** 21–22, 22 (ill.)
Armour, Philip
  **PS:** 165, 166, 166 (ill.)
Armstrong, Samuel C.
  **B:** 230
Art
  **A:** 215–17
Arthur, Chester A.
  **A:** 14, 15 (ill.), 16, 80, 103
  **B:** 13, 14–15, 15 (ill.)
  **PS:** 3
Arts and Crafts movement
  **A:** 218–19
ARU (American Railway Union)
  **A:** 56, 57, 58

Asch building
  **PS:** 197, 198, 200, 201 (ill.),
    206 (ill.)
Ashcan School
  **A:** 217
Ashley, James
  **B:** 45
Asplund, Lillian Gertrud
  **PS:** 226
Assassinations
  **A:** 168
  **B:** 131–32
Assembly lines
  **A:** 252–54, 253 (ill.)
Assimilation
  **A:** 86, 105, 108, 155, 157, 221
  **B:** 19, 185, 197–98
  **PS:** 17–18, 32–33,
    33 (ill.), 37
Atlanta Compromise
  **B:** 233
  **PS:** 99
Audubon Society. *See* National
  Audubon Society
Augusta Tourists
  **B:** 26, 27
Automobiles
  **A:** 224–25, 252–54, 253 (ill.)
Averell, Mary Williamson
  **B:** 76
*The Awakening* (Chopin)
  **A:** 210–11
AWSA (American Woman
  Suffrage Association)
  **A:** 182
  **B:** 207
  **PS:** 74, 76

**B**

Babies. *See* Children and youth
Ballard, Robert
  **PS:** 223
Ballinger, Richard A.
  **A:** 270

Bandelier National Monument
  **PS:** 142, 143 (ill.)
Banking industry
  **A:** 264–65
  **B:** 163–64
Banks
  **B:** 122
Bannan, Benjamin
  **A:** 42–43, 46
Bara, Theda
  **A:** 178, 179 (ill.)
Barbed wire
  **A:** 114, 115 (ill.)
Barnett, Ferdinand L.
  **PS:** 94
Bartholdi, Frédéric Auguste
  **PS:** 21
Baseball
  **A:** 221
  **B:** 25, 26–31
Baseball cards
  **B:** 32–33
Baseball Hall of Fame
  **B:** 25, 31
Batch and custom production. *See*
  Custom and batch production
Batteries
  **B:** 49
Battle of Little Bighorn
  **B:** 183, 186
  **PS:** 14, 15 (ill.), 16, 19
Baum, L. Frank
  **A:** 146–47, 202
  **B:** 209
Bayard-Chamberlain Treaty
  **A:** 156
  **B:** 20
Beaches
  **B:** 199
Beauty Ranch
  **B:** 115–16, 117
Bechet, Sidney
  **A:** 230
Bedicoe Island
  **A:** 69
Beef
  **PS:** 165, 167

Beef industry
    *A:* 263, 264. *See also* Cattle
Beef Trust
    *A:* 263, 264
    *B:* 162, 163
Beer
    *B:* 246–47
Bell, Alexander Graham
    *A:* 248–50, 249 (ill.)
    *B:* 14, 46
Berkman, Alexander
    *A:* 55
    *B:* 57, 58–59, 62, 62 (ill.), 63
Berliner, Emile
    *A:* 229
Bernstein, Samuel
    *PS:* 200
Berryman, Clifford K.
    *B:* 160
BIA (U.S. Bureau of Indian Affairs)
    *A:* 104
Bible
    *B:* 207
    *PS:* 80
Bicycles
    *A:* 243–44
Big business
    custom and batch firms vs.,
        *A:* 24–25, 30
    laissez faire approach, *A:* 37
    Pinkerton National Detective
        Agency, *A:* 46
    Roosevelt, Theodore, vs.,
        *A:* 260, 261
    strategies, *A:* 26–28, 30–31
Big Foot (Native American tribal
    chief)
    *A:* 109–10
Big Steve. *See* Cleveland, Grover
Big Stick diplomacy
    *A:* 262, 267 (ill.)
    *B:* 158
Billy the Kid
    *A:* 117
Bimetallism
    *A:* 143, 163

    *B:* 122–23, 124, 125
Bird and Game Act of 1900
    *PS:* 140
Birth control
    *A:* 174–75
    *B:* 60, 61 (ill.)
*The Birth Control Review*
    (publication)
    *A:* 175
*Birth of a Nation* (Griffith)
    *A:* 228
Bison. *See* Buffalo
Black Americans. *See* African
    Americans
Black Codes. *See also* Jim
    Crow laws
    *PS:* 87
Black Coyote
    *A:* 110
Black Friday
    *B:* 65, 68, 70
Black Hills
    *PS:* 14
Blackface
    *A:* 226, 227
Blacks. *See* African Americans
Blackwell, Henry
    *PS:* 74
Blaine, James
    *A:* 16–17, 18, 150,
        151–52
    *B:* 12–13, 88 (ill.), 88–89
Blanck, Max
    *PS:* 197, 207, 208
Bland-Allison Act of 1878
    *A:* 12
BLF (Brotherhood of Locomotive
    Firemen)
    *A:* 58
Blizzards
    *A:* 92
Blues music
    *A:* 229–30
Bly, Nellie
    *A:* 220
    *B:* 59–60

Board of Education (Chicago,
    Illinois)
    *B:* 7
Bonds, government. *See*
    Government bonds
Bonney, William Henry. *See* Billy
    the Kid
*The Book of Modern Homes and
    Building Plans*
    *A:* 209
    *PS:* 176
Boone and Crockett Club
    *A:* 122
Borden, Lizzie
    *A:* 220
*Boston* (Sinclair)
    *A:* 213
    *B:* 180–81
Boxer Rebellion
    *A:* 168
    *B:* 131
Boxing
    *A:* 222–24
Boy Scouts
    *B:* 99
Boycotts
    *A:* 56, 142
Boys' clubs
    *B:* 81
Boys' weeklies
    *B:* 174
Brace, Charles Loring
    *PS:* 63
Breaker Boys
    *A:* 189–91, 193 (ill.)
    *PS:* 125–35, 131 (ill.), 133 (ill.)
Breakers (mansion)
    *B:* 227 (ill.)
Brentwood (Sears Modern Home
    Numbers 13394C and
    13394D)
    *PS:* 190 (ill.)
Brewing industry
    *B:* 246–47
Brewster, Benjamin
    *PS:* 157

Britain. *See* Great Britain
British Columbia
    *B:* 77, 78
"The Bronco Buster" (artwork)
    *PS:* 44 (ill.)
Brotherhood of Locomotive
    Firemen (BLF)
    *A:* 58
Brown, Henry Billings
    *PS:* 100, 100 (ill.)
Brown, James Joseph
    *PS:* 218
Brown, Leola
    *PS:* 104 (ill.)
Brown, Linda
    *PS:* 103, 104 (ill.)
Brown, Margaret Tobin
    (Unsinkable Molly Brown)
    *PS:* 218 (ill.), 218–19
Brown, Molly. *See* Brown,
    Margaret Tobin (Unsinkable
    Molly Brown)
Brown, Oliver
    *PS:* 103, 104 (ill.)
Brown, Terry Lynn
    *PS:* 104 (ill.)
*Brown v. Board of Education*
    *PS:* 103, 104 (ill.)
Bryan, William Jennings
    anti-imperialism, *B:* 128
    antitrust viewpoint, *A:* 35
    monetary policy, *A:* 143–45,
        144 (ill.)
    presidential election of 1896,
        *A:* 163; *B:* 23, 121,
        122 (ill.), 122–23, 124–25
    presidential election of 1900,
        *A:* 168; *B:* 131
    presidential election of 1904,
        *B:* 160–61
    presidential election of 1908,
        *A:* 269; *B:* 168
    Scopes Trial, *B:* 123
    *Wizard of Oz* reference to,
        *A:* 147
Budget and Accounting Act of 1921
    *A:* 272

Budget, federal. *See* Federal
    budget
Buffalo
    *A:* 101, 111, 113 (ill.)
    *PS:* 13, 18, 18 (ill.), 42
Buffalo Bill. *See* Cody, William
    (Buffalo Bill)
"Buffalo Bill's Wild West"
    (performance)
    *A:* 106–7, 107 (ill.)
Buffalo Soldiers
    *A:* 101, 257–58, 269
    *B:* 154
Bull Moose Party. *See* Progressive
    Party
Bungalows
    *PS:* 178, 185 (ill.), 187 (ill.)
Buntline, Ned
    *A:* 106
Bureau of Indian Affairs (BIA)
    *A:* U.S., 104
Bureau of Personal Service
    *B:* 198
Bureau of the Census, U.S.
    *A:* 110–11
Burroughs, John
    *B:* 77
Busch, Adolphus
    *B:* 113
Bush, George W.
    *A:* 12 (ill.), 12–13
Bush, Jeb
    *A:* 12
Business ethics
    *PS:* 151, 152–58
Butler Act
    *B:* 123
Butler, Benjamin
    *A:* 9

## C

Cable cars
    *A:* 95, 96 (ill.)
California
    *B:* 138, 139

    *PS:* 148
California Club
    *A:* 123
California Gold Rush of 1849
    *B:* 223–24
*The Call of the Wild* (London)
    *B:* 114–15
Cameras
    *A:* 251–52
    *B:* 49–50
Cameron, James
    *PS:* 224
Campaign contributions
    *A:* 263
    *B:* 161
Campbell, Alexander
    *A:* 47–48
Canada
    *A:* 156, 233–37, 239–41
    *B:* 19–20, 186
Canals
    *B:* 165–66
Candy industry
    *B:* 32–33
Canneries
    *PS:* 126–27
Capitalism
    *A:* 278
    *B:* 175
Carbon monoxide
    *PS:* 173
Carnegie, Andrew
    *PS:* 51–59, 52 (ill.)
    anti-imperialism, *B:* 128
    big business, *A:* 30
    "The Gospel of Wealth,"
        *A:* 31, 31 (ill.), 171–72; *PS:*
        53–56
    Homestead Strike, *A:* 54–56;
        *B:* 57–58, 59
    industrialization, *A:* 24
    philanthropy of, *A:* 196, 219;
        *B:* 226, 232; *PS:* 56–58
    robber baron, *A:* 26;
        *PS:* 52–53, 159 (ill.)
Carnegie Corporation
    *PS:* 56

Carnegie Hall
 *PS:* 56, 57 (ill.), 58 (ill.)
Carnegie Steel Company
 *A:* 23–24, 30, 35, 54–56
 *B:* 57–59
Carow, Edith Kermit
 *B:* 152
*Carpathia* (ship)
 *PS:* 216, 217 (ill.), 219–20,
 221
Carpetbaggers
 *A:* 3
Carter, Jimmy
 *B:* 166
 *PS:* 147
Cartoons, political. *See also* Nast,
 Thomas
 *A:* 206–7
Cassant, Mary
 *A:* 216–17
Cassidy, Butch
 *A:* 118
Catalogs
 *A:* 208–9
 *PS:* 175, 176, 177, 177 (ill.)
Catholics. *See* Roman Catholicism
Catt, Carrie Chapman
 *PS:* 74 (ill.), 75, 75 (ill.)
Cattle. *See also* Beef industry
 *A:* 113, 114, 115 (ill.)
Cedars (Sears Modern Home
 Number C3278)
 *PS:* 189 (ill.)
*The Celebrated Jumping Frog of
 Calaveras County; and Other
 Sketches* (Twain)
 *B:* 213
Census, U.S. Bureau of the
 *A:* 110–11
Central Pacific Railroad (CPR)
 *A:* 78
Central Railroad of Georgia
 *B:* 80
*A Century of Dishonor* (Jackson)
 *A:* 103
*The Century* (publication)
 *PS:* 108

Chafin, Eugene W.
 *B:* 170
Chaney, William Henry
 *B:* 112
Charity. *See* Philanthropy
Charles L. Webster Company
 *B:* 215
Chase, Andrew
 *PS:* 165
Chautauqua
 *B:* 216, 217
Chelsea (Sears Modern Home
 Number 111)
 *PS:* 180 (ill.)
Chewing gum
 *B:* 33
Chicago Board of Education. *See*
 Board of Education (Chicago,
 Illinois)
Chicago, Burlington & Quincy
 Railroad
 *B:* 80
Chicago, Illinois
 *A:* 200
 *PS:* 165, 166, 170, 173
 Haymarket Square riot, *B:* 55
 Hull-House, *B:* 1, 4, 7
 meatpacking industry, *B:* 100
 school segregation, *B:* 242
 Solomon, Hannah,
  *B:* 193–95, 198, 199
 Wells-Barnett, Ida B.,
  *B:* 241–43
 women activists, *B:* 200
Chicago Negro School of Ballet
 *B:* 200
Chicago School of Civics and
 Philanthropy
 *B:* 7
*Chicago Sunday Tribune*
 *PS:* 202–4
Chicago Woman's Club (CWC),
 *B:* 194–95
Chicago Women's City Club
 *B:* 199
Chicago World's Fair.
 *See* Columbian Exposition

Child abuse and neglect
 *PS:* 64–67
Child labor. *See also* Breaker Boys
 *A:* 188–93, 192 (ill.), 193 (ill.)
 *B:* 96–99, 98 (ill.), 99 (ill.),
 195
 agriculture, *PS:* 126
 canneries, *PS:* 126–27
 coal mining, *PS:* 125–35, 131
 (ill.), 133 (ill.)
 cotton mills, *PS:* 127
 factories, *PS:* 126
 garment industry, *PS:* 70, 127
 newsies, *PS:* 127
 tobacco industry, *PS:* 126,
 128 (ill.)
Children and youth. *See also*
 Child abuse and neglect;
 Child labor
 *PS:* 64–67, 65 (ill.), 69
 Hull-House, *B:* 6 (ill.)
 social reform for,
  *B:* 195
 Wald, Lillian, *B:* 5
*Children of the Poor* (Riis)
 *B:* 100
*Children of the Tenements* (Riis)
 *B:* 100
Children's Bureau, U.S.
 *B:* 5
Chile
 *A:* 159
 *B:* 87
Chilkoot Pass
 *A:* 236–37, 238
China
 *A:* 167–68, 268
 *B:* 130–31, 166–67
Chinaman, John. *See* John
 Chinaman
Chinatown
 *A:* 77
 *PS:* 3, 11
Chinese Consolidated Benevolent
 Association. *See* Chinese Six
 Companies

Chinese Exclusion Act of 1882
  *A:* 80–82, 81 (ill.), 157–58,
    165
  *B:* 14, 84, 127
  *PS:* 1–12
  background, *PS:* 1–3, 5–6
  ramifications of, *PS:* 10
  text of, *PS:* 6–10
Chinese Six Companies
  *A:* 79
  *PS:* 3
Chopin, Kate
  *A:* 210–11
Christianity
  *B:* 60, 198, 207, 209
"Chrysanthemum" ( Joplin)
  *B:* 108
Cigar Makers International Union
  *A:* 53
Cigarette industry. *See* Tobacco
  industry
Cigar-making industry
  *A:* 53
Citizens' Committee
  *PS:* 98
Civil rights
  *A:* 1–3
  *B:* 233–34
  *PS:* 77
Civil Rights Act of 1875
  *A:* 139
Civil service
  *A:* 7, 14, 16, 153, 154 (ill.), 165
  *B:* 15, 128
Civil Service Commission, U.S.
  *B:* 14, 153
Civil War, U.S. *See* American
  Civil War
Clark, John J.
  *A:* 68
Clark, William
  *A:* 119
Classes, social. *See* Social classes
Clayton Anti-Trust Act of 1914
  *A:* 278
Clemens, Samuel. *See* Twain,
  Mark

Cleveland, Frances
  *B:* 16–17, 17 (ill.)
**Cleveland, Grover**
  *B:* 11 (ill.), **11–24,** 17 (ill.)
  *PS:* 21
  Dawes Severalty Act, *B:* 19
  early years, *B:* 11–12
  economic policy, *B:* 20–21
  foreign affairs, *B:* 19–20, 22–23
  Harrison, Benjamin, *B:* 85
  immigration policy, *A:* 82
  Interstate Commerce Act,
    *B:* 18–19
  interstate commerce policy,
    *A:* 29
  labor movement, *A:* 162 (ill.)
  marriage, *B:* 16–17
  monetary policy, *A:* 129 (ill.),
    143
  monopoly opposition, *A:* 33
  Mugwumps, *A:* 8 (ill.)
  patronage reform, *B:* 13–16,
    128
  political beginnings, *B:* 12
  presidency overview,
    *A:* 149–57, 152 (ill.),
    154 (ill.), 160–63
  presidential election of 1884,
    *A:* 16–18, 19 (ill.)
  presidential election of 1888,
    *A:* 19 (ill.)
  presidential election of 1892,
    *A:* 19 (ill.), 142; *B:* 90–91
  presidential election of 1896,
    *B:* 121
  Pullman strike, *A:* 57;
    *B:* 21–22, 23
  tariffs, *A:* 136–38
Cleveland Indians
  *B:* 30–31
Cleveland, Ohio
  *PS:* 156–58
Cleveland, Oscar Folsom
  *A:* 151
  *B:* 13
Cleveland, Rose
  *B:* 16

Clinton, Bill
  *PS:* 147
Coal mining
  *B:* 157–58
  Breaker Boys, *PS:* 125–35,
    131 (ill.), 133 (ill.)
  children, *A:* 189–91,
    192 (ill.), 193 (ill.)
  labor movement, *A:* 39–48,
    60–63, 62 (ill.), 260–61
  wages, *PS:* 135
Coal Strike Conference of 1902
  *B:* 157
**Cobb, Ty**
  *B:* 25 (ill.), **25–34,** 29 (ill.),
    33 (ill.)
  baseball career, *B:* 26–31
  early years, *B:* 25–26
  later years, *B:* 31–33
Coca-Cola
  *A:* 220
Cocaine
  *A:* 210
Cody, William (Buffalo Bill)
  *A:* 106–7, 107 (ill.)
  *B:* 187, 190 (ill.)
Colby, Leonard
  *B:* 190–91
Collecting
  *B:* 32–33
Collective security
  *B:* 88
Collusion
  *A:* 29
Colombia
  *B:* 165–66
Colorado
  *PS:* 38
Colorado Fuel & Iron Company
  *A:* 63
Colored Americans. *See* African
  Americans
Colored Farmers' Alliance
  *A:* 141–42
Columbia University
  *B:* 5, 39

Columbian Exposition
  *A:* 204 (ill.), 218
  *B:* 196, 200, 241
  *PS:* 83–94, 84 (ill.), 92 (ill.)
"Combination March" (Joplin)
  *B:* 106
Commerce and Labor, U.S.
  Department of
  *B:* 158
Commercial Bureau of American
  Republics
  *B:* 88
Communism
  *B:* 89, 131
Competition
  *A:* 32
  *B:* 222–24
Compromise of 1877
  *A:* 11
"Compromise with the South"
  (Nast)
  *B:* 143, 144 (ill.)
Comstock Law of 1873
  *A:* 174
Congress. *See* U.S. Congress
Conkling, Roscoe
  *A:* 13, 14, 14 (ill.), 15–16
  *B:* 14
Conscription. *See* Military draft
Conservation movement
  Harrison, Benjamin, *A:* 159
  overview, *A:* 120–24
  Pinchot, Gifford, *A:* 270
  in Progressive Era, *PS:* 144
  Roosevelt, Theodore,
    *A:* 261–62, 268–69, 270;
    *PS:* 47–48, 140
Conservationism
  *B:* 133, 136, 158–59, 164
Conspicuous consumption
  *A:* 202
Conspiracies
  *B:* 189–91
Consumerism
  *A:* 25, 202, 206–7
Contamination, food. *See* Food
  safety

Contraception. *See* Birth control
Contributions, campaign
  *A:* 263
Convict lease system
  *PS:* 87, 89
Cook, Frederick
  *A:* 254
Cooke, Jay
  *A:* 49
Coolidge, Calvin
  *A:* 176
Coolies. *See also* Immigrants and
  immigration
  *PS:* 2–3
Cooper, Anderson
  *B:* 227
Cooper, James Fenimore
  *A:* 119
  *PS:* 34
Corbin, Abel Rathbone
  *B:* 69–70
Corporate ethics
  *A:* 32
Corruption in government
  *B:* 13–16, 144–45
  Cleveland, Grover, on, *A:* 153
  Native American affairs,
    *A:* 101, 103
  patronage, *A:* 7
  Tammany Hall, *A:* 4–5
Corsets
  *PS:* 121–22
Cottages
  *PS:* 183 (ill.)
Cottons mills
  *PS:* 127
Cowboys
  *PS:* 48
Coxey, Jacob
  *A:* 131, 147
CPR (Central Pacific Railroad)
  *A:* 78
Cracker Jack
  *B:* 32–33
Crafton (Sears Modern Home
  Number 3318)
  *PS:* 192 (ill.)

Crazy Horse
  *B:* 185, 186
  *PS:* 14
Creelman, James
  *PS:* 14–15
Crime
  *A:* 97, 116–18
Croker, Edward
  *PS:* 203, 206
Croydon (Sears Modern Home
  Number 13718)
  *PS:* 191 (ill.)
*Crusade for Justice* (Wells-Barnett)
  *B:* 243
Cuba
  *A:* 19, 161, 167, 168,
    257–58
  *B:* 23, 129–30, 153–55, 165
Currency. *See also* Gold; Silver
  *B:* 121
Currency policy. *See* Monetary
  policy
Currier and Ives
  *B:* 248 (ill.)
Curtis, Edward
  *B:* 78
Custer, George Armstrong
  *B:* 185, 186
  *PS:* 14, 15 (ill.), 16, 19
Custer's Last Stand. *See* Battle of
  Little Bighorn
Custom and batch production
  *A:* 24–25, 27–28, 30
CWC (Chicago Woman's Club),
  194–95
Czolgosz, Leon
  *A:* 168
  *B:* 60, 131, 132

**D**

Dakota Territory
  *PS:* 42, 46
Darrow, Clarence
  *B:* 123

Darwin, Charles
  *A:* 31
  *PS:* 53
"A Daughter of the South" (artwork)
  *PS:* 117 (ill.)
Davis, David
  *A:* 10–11
Dawes, Henry L.
  *A:* 105
  *PS:* 34, 35 (ill.)
Dawes Severalty Act
  *A:* 17, 103, 105, 108, 154,
    155, 157
  *B:* 18, 19
  *PS:* 31–39
  excerpt, *PS:* 35–37
  failure of, *PS:* 17–18, 37–38
  land conflicts preceding,
    *PS:* 31–34
  stipulations, *PS:* 34–35
Debs, Eugene
  *A:* 56, 57, 58–59, 59 (ill.), 61
  *B:* 170
Debt
  *A:* 131–32
Declaration of Sentiments
  *B:* 205
Deflation
  *A:* 7, 9
Democratic Party
  *B:* 13, 14–15, 21, 147
  Cleveland, Grover,
    *A:* 160–61, 162–63
  during Gilded Age, *A:* 3–7
  presidential election of 1876,
    *A:* 10–11
  presidential election of 1880,
    *A:* 15
  presidential election of 1884,
    *A:* 17
  presidential election of 1888,
    *A:* 18
  presidential election of 1896,
    *A:* 143–45
  presidential election of 1904,
    *A:* 263
  tariff policy, *A:* 136–38

Demonstrations and protests
  *A:* 131
  *PS:* 74 (ill.)
Denver Woman's Club
  *PS:* 218
Department of Agriculture, U.S.
  *A:* 123, 124
  *B:* 164
  *PS:* 172
Department of Commerce and
  Labor, U.S.
  *B:* 158
Department of Labor, U.S.
  *B:* 123
Department of the Interior, U.S.
  *B:* 164
  *PS:* 142
Depression, economic. *See*
  Economic depressions
Depression, Great. *See* Great
  Depression
Desegregation
  *PS:* 103
Detroit Tigers
  *B:* 27–28, 30–31
Devil's Tower (Wyoming)
  *PS:* 145, 146 (ill.)
**Dewey, John**
  *A:* 194
  *B:* 35 (ill.), **35–41**
  criticism of, *B:* 40–41
  early years, *B:* 36–37
  Hine, Lewis, *B:* 94
  laboratory school,
    *B:* 37–39
  later years, *B:* 39
  pragmatism, *B:* 35, 37
DiCaprio, Leonardo
  *PS:* 224, 225 (ill.)
Dickinson, Emily
  *A:* 102
Dickson, William K. L.
  *B:* 49, 50
Dime novels
  *A:* 214–15
  *B:* 174

Dimmick, Mary Scott Lord
  *B:* 91
Dingley, Nelson R.
  *A:* 163
  *B:* 127
Dingley Tariff Act of 1897
  *A:* 163–64
  *B:* 127
Discrimination, racial. *See* Racism
Disease
  *A:* 67–69, 74
Division of Forestry, U.S.
  *See* National Forest Service
Divorce
  *A:* 175, 177
"Dr. Dodge's Wife Tells Story of
  *Titanic* Wreck" (Dodge)
  *PS:* 214–20
Dodge, Ruth
  *PS:* 211–26
Dodge, Washington
  *PS:* 214, 223
Dole, Sanford B.
  *A:* 166 (ill.)
Dolliver, Jonathan Prentiss
  *PS:* 139
Dominican Republic
  *B:* 165
Douglass, Frederick
  *A:* 203
  *B:* 233, 241
  *PS:* 85, 86
Draft, military. *See* Military draft
*Dragon's Teeth* (Sinclair)
  *B:* 181
*Drawings*
  *PS:* 108
Drew, Daniel
  *B:* 67, 68, 225
Drug abuse
  *A:* 210
Drugs
  *B:* 177
Du Bois, W. E. B.
  *A:* 212–13, 275
  *B:* 233–34
  *PS:* 99

Duchamp, Marcel
  *A:* 217
Dunbar, Paul Lawrence
  *PS:* 85
Dunham, Katherine
  *B:* 200
DuPont
  *B:* 163
Dupuy de Lôme, Enrique
  *A:* 167
  *B:* 154

## E

E. H. Harriman Award
  *B:* 81
Earthquakes
  *B:* 112, 113, 113 (ill.), 134–35
Eastman, George
  *A:* 251–52
Eckley Miners' Village
  (Stroudsburg, Pennsylvania)
  *A:* 41, 42 (ill.)
Economic depressions. *See also*
  Great Depression
  *A:* 33, 127–33, 160
  *B:* 20–21, 23, 121
Edison Electric Light Company
  *B:* 47–48
Edison General Electric
  *B:* 48
**Edison, Thomas**
  *A:* 229, 250
  *B:* 43 (ill.), **43–51,** 46 (ill.)
  early years, *B:* 43–44
  electric light system, *B:* 47–48
  later years, *B:* 50–51
  Miller, Lewis, *B:* 217
  phonograph, *B:* 48–49,
    49 (ill.)
  telegraph, *B:* 44–47
  Twain, Mark, *B:* 219
Education
  African Americans, *A:* 195
  Native American, *A:* 103–4;
    *PS:* 17

philanthropy, *A:* 219
reform, *A:* 193–96
segregation, *PS:* 102–3
women's, *A:* 177
Educational philosophy
  *B:* 35, 37–39, 40–41, 233
*Edward Henry Harriman* (Muir)
  *B:* 81
Edwards, Sarah
  *B:* 143
The Eight
  *A:* 217
Eighteenth Amendment
  *A:* 145
  *B:* 249
*Eighty Years and More* (Stanton)
  *B:* 206
Einstein, Albert
  *A:* 254
Elections, presidential.
  *See* Presidential elections
Elections, primary. *See* Primary
  elections
Electoral votes. *See also*
  Presidential elections
  *A:* 151, 263
  *B:* 85, 125, 161
Electric lamps
  *A:* 250
Electricity
  *A:* 23, 250–51
Elevators, grain. *See* Grain elevators
Elkins Act of 1903
  *A:* 262
  *B:* 158
Ellis Island
  *A:* 67 (ill.), 68–69, 69 (ill.)
  *B:* 95 (ill.), 95–96
  *PS:* 21, 27, 28, 28 (ill.)
Ellwood, Isaac
  *A:* 114
Elsmore (Sears Modern Home
  Numbers 208 and 2013)
  *PS:* 187 (ill.)
Emancipation of slaves
  *PS:* 87, 97

Emancipation Proclamation
  *B:* 237
  *PS:* 97
Emerson, Ralph Waldo
  *A:* 120
  *B:* 135
  *PS:* 24
Empire State Building
  *B:* 101, 102 (ill.)
Employees, government. *See* Civil
  service
"The Entertainer" (Joplin)
  *B:* 107
Entertainment
  *A:* 106–7, 107 (ill.), 225–26
Environmental cleanup
  *B:* 199
Equal protection
  *PS:* 97, 98, 103
Erdman Act of 1898
  *A:* 57, 165
Erie Railroad
  *A:* 32
  *B:* 67–69, 225, 226 (ill.)
Erie Ring
  *B:* 68
Erie War
  *B:* 225
Essays
  *A:* 120–21
Ethics, business
  *PS:* 151, 152–58
Ethics, political
  *A:* 4–5
Ethnic violence
  *PS:* 24
Eugenics
  *A:* 31, 175, 176
Evolution
  *B:* 123
Exile
  *B:* 63
Expansionism. *See also* Anti-
  imperialism; Territorial
  expansion
  *A:* 165–67, 168, 265

Experimental schools
A: 194
Explorers
A: 119
Exports
B: 20

**F**

*The Fabric of My Life* (Solomon)
B: 193
Factories. *See* Industrialization
Factory Investigating Commission
(New York City)
PS: 207
Fair Labor Standards Act of 1938
A: 193
PS: 135
Fairbanks, Charles W.
A: 263
B: 161
Fairs
A: 200–204, 204 (ill.)
PS: 83–94
Family planning. *See* Birth control
Famine, Potato. *See* Potato Famine
Farm Security Administration
(FSA)
B: 102
Farm tenancy. *See* Tenancy
Farmers and farming. *See also*
Agriculture
B: 121, 124
Fashion
flapper, PS: 120–21, 121 (ill.)
Gibson Girl, PS: 107,
109–11, 114 (ill.), 116 (ill.),
118 (ill.), 121–22
FBI (Federal Bureau of
Investigation)
A: 220
FDA (U.S. Food and Drug
Administration)
PS: 171
Federal budget
A: 271–72

Federal Bureau of Investigation
(FBI)
A: 220
Federal Children's Bureau. *See*
U.S. Children's Bureau
Federal Land Grant Program
A: 116
Federal Reserve Act of 1913
A: 278
Federal Reserve System
A: 265
B: 164
Federal Trade Commission Act
of 1914
A: 278
Federal Trade Commission (FTC)
A: 34–35
Feminism
A: 178–79
B: 7, 60, 178–79, 207
Fences
A: 114, 115 (ill.)
Ferguson, John H.
PS: 98
*Ferguson, Plessy v.,* court case.
*See Plessy v. Ferguson*
Feudalism
A: 26
Ferris, George Washington Gale
PS: 93
Ferris Wheel
PS: 93
Field, Cyrus
A: 27 (ill.)
Fifteenth Amendment
A: 182
B: 207
PS: 97
Fillmore, Millard
A: 76
Films. *See* Motion pictures
Fire, Triangle Shirtwaist
PS: 197–208, 201 (ill.),
205 (ill.), 206 (ill.)
Fires. *See also* Fire, Triangle
Shirtwaist
B: 113 (ill.)

Fishing rights
A: 156
B: 19–20
Fisk, James
B: 67, 68, 69–70, 225,
226 (ill.)
Fjords
B: 79
Flager, Henry Morrison
PS: 155
Flagg, James Montgomery
PS: 120, 120 (ill.)
Flappers
PS: 120–21, 121 (ill.)
Florida
A: 12–13
Florida Supreme Court
A: 13
Folklore
A: 118–19
Folsom, Emma
B: 16
Folsom, Frances. *See* Cleveland,
Frances
Folsom, Oscar
B: 13
Food and Drug Act of 1906. *See*
Pure Food and Drug Act of 1906
Food and Drug Administration,
U.S.
PS: 171
Food safety
B: 162–63, 177–78, 180 (ill.)
PS: 165, 166, 167, 168–72,
173
Ford, Bob
A: 117
Ford, Charlie
A: 117
Ford, Henry
A: 224–25, 225 (ill.)
B: 50
Ford Motor Company
A: 252–54, 253 (ill.)
Foreign aid
A: 272

Foreign policy
  Cleveland, Grover, *A:* 156, 161
  Harrison, Benjamin, *A:* 159
  McKinley, William, *A:* 167–68
  Roosevelt, Theodore, *A:* 262, 265
  Taft, William Howard, *A:* 272
Foreign trade. *See* International trade
*The Forerunner* (publication)
  *B:* 179
Forest Service, U.S. *See* National Forest Service
Forestry
  *A:* 122–24, 268–69
Forestry, U.S. Division of. *See* National Forest Service
Forests
  *B:* 164
Forsyth, James
  *A:* 110
Fort Laramie Treaty of 1868
  *B:* 185
  *PS:* 14
Fourteen Points
  *A:* 278–79
Fourteenth Amendment
  *PS:* 74, 97, 98, 103
France
  *PS:* 223–24
*Frank Leslie's Illustrated Newspaper*
  *B:* 142
Fraser, James Earle
  *PS:* 18
Free Silver movement
  *B:* 122
Free silver policy. *See* Bimetallism
Freedom of speech
  *B:* 60
Frelinghuysen-Zavala Treaty
  *A:* 156
French Research Institute for Exploitation of the Sea (IFREMER)
  *PS:* 223
Freud, Sigmund
  *A:* 254

Frick, Henry Clay
  *A:* 55–56
  *B:* 58–59, 161
Froelich, Ralph A.
  *PS:* 204
Frontier, American. *See* American Frontier; American West
FSA (Farm Security Administration)
  *B:* 102
FTC (Federal Trade Commission)
  *A:* 34–35
Fuller, Meta
  *B:* 174
Fulton, Robert
  *B:* 222

**G**

Gage, Matilda Joslyn
  *B:* 206, 207, 208 (ill.), 208–9
Gardener, Helen
  *PS:* 81 (ill.)
Garfield, James A.
  *A:* 13–16, 15 (ill.)
  *B:* 15 (ill.)
  Blaine, James G., *B:* 13
  Harrison, Benjamin, *B:* 84
  patronage, *B:* 14
  presidential election of 1880, *B:* 89
Garment industry
  *A:* 85
  *PS:* 70, 127, 197–200, 205–7
Garrett, Pat
  *A:* 117
General Allotment Act. *See* Dawes Severalty Act
General Electric
  *B:* 48
George, Henry
  *A:* 183
*George W. Elder* (ship)
  *B:* 77
Georgia Peach. *See* Cobb, Ty
Gerckens, Laurence
  *A:* 184–85

Geronimo
  *B:* 188 (ill.), 188–89
Ghost Dance
  *A:* 108–9, 109 (ill.)
  *B:* 187
Gibbons, Thomas
  *B:* 222, 223
Gibson, Charles Dana
  *A:* 223
  *PS:* 107–23, 109 (ill.)
  "A Daughter of the South," *PS:* 117 (ill.)
  early years, *PS:* 107–8
  Gibson Girl, *PS:* 108–11
  Gibson Girl drawing number 1, *PS:* 115 (ill.)
  Gibson Girl illustration on stamp, *PS:* 119 (ill.)
  "The Greatest Game in the World—His Move," *PS:* 112 (ill.)
  impact of, *PS:* 120–22
  Nesbit, Evelyn, *PS:* 110 (ill.)
  "Not Worrying About Her Rights," *PS:* 118 (ill.)
  "Picturesque America— Anywhere Along the Coast," *PS:* 116 (ill.)
  "The Question Mark," *PS:* 113 (ill.)
  "Studies in Expression— When Women Are Jurors," *PS:* 114 (ill.)
  "The Weaker Sex," *PS:* 114 (ill.)
Gibson Girl
  *A:* 223, 223 (ill.)
  "A Daughter of the South," *PS:* 117 (ill.)
  Gibson Girl drawing number 1, *PS:* 115 (ill.)
  Gibson Girl illustration on stamp, *PS:* 119 (ill.)
  "The Greatest Game in the World—His Move," *PS:* 112 (ill.)

Nesbit, Evelyn, *PS:* 110 (ill.)
"Not Worrying About Her
  Rights," *PS:* 118 (ill.)
"Picturesque America—
  Anywhere Along the
  Coast," *PS:* 116 (ill.)
"The Question Mark,"
  *PS:* 113 (ill.)
"Studies in Expression—
  When Women Are Jurors,"
  *PS:* 114 (ill.)
"The Weaker Sex,"
  *PS:* 114 (ill.)
Gibson Man
  *PS:* 109, 112 (ill.)
Gilded Age
  advertising, *A:* 204–5, 206–7
  agriculture, *A:* 130–35
  architecture, *A:* 218
  art, *A:* 215–17
  consumerism, *A:* 205
  defined, *A:* 3
  economic depression,
    *A:* 127–33
  entertainment, *A:* 225–26
  fairs, *A:* 200–204
  gold prospecting, *A:* 233–37,
    239–41
  immigration, *A:* 65–98
  industrialization, *A:* 21–37
  inventions, *A:* 248–54
  labor movement, *A:* 39–64
  literature, *A:* 207–13
  motion pictures, *A:* 227–28
  music, *A:* 228–30
  newspapers, *A:* 213–15
  philanthropy, *A:* 219
  photography, *A:* 217–18
  political aspects, *A:* 3–20,
    133–36
  political cartoons, *A:* 206–7
  populism, *A:* 138, 141–45,
    146–47
  presidential leadership,
    *A:* 149–69
  racism, *A:* 138–41

  sports, *A:* 219–25
  tariffs, *A:* 136–38
  temperance movement, *A:* 145
  westward expansion, *A:* 99–125
  Wright brothers, *A:* 241–47
*The Gilded Age* (Twain and Warner)
  *A:* 209–10
  *B:* 214
Gillett, Frederick
  *PS:* 81 (ill.)
Gilman, Charlotte Perkins
  *B:* 176–77, 178 (ill.),
    178–79
Girl Scouts
  *B:* 99
Glaciers
  *B:* 78–79, 134–35
Gladden, Washington
  *A:* 219
Glidden, Joseph
  *A:* 114
Göbel, Heinrich
  *A:* 250
Gold
  Cleveland, Grover, *B:* 21
  Gould, Jay, *B:* 69–70
  McKinley, William, *B:* 125
  Populist Party, *B:* 122–23,
    124–25
  prospecting, *B:* 114
  Sherman Silver Purchase Act,
    *B:* 87
Gold and Stock Telegraph
  Company
  *B:* 45
Gold Indicator Company
  *B:* 44–45
Gold policy
  bimetallism, *A:* 143
  Bryan, William Jennings,
    *A:* 144, 144 (ill.)
  Cleveland, Grover, *A:* 160–61
  economic depression,
    *A:* 127–28, 129
  Harrison, Benjamin, *A:* 158–59
  McKinley, William, *A:* 163

Gold prospecting
  *A:* 77, 234–35, 237 (ill.),
    239–41, 240 (ill.)
  *PS:* 1
Gold Standard Act of 1900
  *A:* 163
  *B:* 126
**Goldman, Emma**
  *B:* 53 (ill.), **53–64,** 61 (ill.),
    62 (ill.)
  activism, *B:* 59–63
  anarchism, *B:* 53, 55–57,
    59–60
  early years, *B:* 54–55
  Homestead Strike of 1892,
    *B:* 57–59
Gompers, Samuel
  *A:* 53–54, 54 (ill.), 57
Goodwin & Co.
  *B:* 32
GOP (Grand Old Party). *See*
  Republican Party
Gordon, Anna
  *B:* 247, 247 (ill.), 249
Gore, Al
  *A:* 12 (ill.), 12–13
"The Gospel of Wealth" (Carnegie)
  *A:* 31, 171–72
  *PS:* 53–56
Goudey
  *B:* 33
**Gould, Jay**
  *A:* 27, 27 (ill.), 32, 51
  *B:* 65 (ill.), **65–73**
  *PS:* 52, 156
  Black Friday, *B:* 69–70
  early years, *B:* 65–67
  Great Southwest Strike, *B:* 71
  legacy, *B:* 72
  railroads, *B:* 67–69, 70 (ill.),
    70–71
  Vanderbilt, Cornelius, *B:* 225
Government assistance
  *A:* 17, 160, 173–74
Government bonds
  *A:* 160–61
  *B:* 21

Government corruption. *See* Corruption in government

Government employees. *See* Civil service

Government reform
*B:* 13–16, 128, 153
civil service, *A:* 165
Cleveland, Grover, *A:* 153, 154 (ill.)
Native American affairs, *A:* 102–4
Roosevelt, Theodore, *A:* 259–60, 263–64, 269
Taft, William Howard, *A:* 271–72
Wilson, Woodrow, *A:* 277–78

Government regulation. *See also* Antitrust actions
*B:* 156–58, 161–62, 162–63
advertising, *A:* 205
big business, *A:* 37
food safety, *PS:* 171–72
grain elevators, *A:* 135
immigration, *A:* 80–82; *PS:* 3, 5–10, 27
railroads, *A:* 29–30, 154–55

Government service. *See* Civil service

Government spending
*B:* 91

Governmental reform. *See* Government reform

Gowen, Franklin
*A:* 43–45, 46, 48

Goyakla. *See* Geronimo

Grain elevators
*A:* 133–35

Gramophones
*A:* 229

Grand Canyon
*PS:* 146

Grand Island Railroad
*B:* 80–81

Grand Old Party (GOP). *See* Republican Party

Grange
*A:* 9, 133–35

Grant, Ulysses S.
*A:* 10, 13, 14, 29
*B:* 69–70, 215, 217

Grants, land
*A:* 114–16

Gray, David
*A:* 225

Gray, Samuel Ward
*PS:* 25

Great Britain
*A:* 156, 161, 268
*B:* 19–20, 22–23

"Great Collision March" (Joplin)
*B:* 106

Great Depression
*B:* 103
*PS:* 193

Great Northern Railroad
*B:* 80

Great Railroad Strike
*A:* 49–51, 50 (ill.)

Great Southwest Strike
*B:* 71

"The Greatest Game in the World—His Move" (artwork)
*PS:* 112 (ill.)

Greenback Party
*A:* 9–10, 15, 135

Greenbacks
*B:* 69

Griffin, Marion Lucy Mahoney
*B:* 200

Griffith, D. W.
*A:* 228

Grinnell, George Bird
*B:* 78

Guam
*A:* 19, 167
*B:* 164

Guerrilla warfare
*B:* 130

*A Guest of Honor* (Joplin)
*B:* 107–8

Guiteau, Charles
*A:* 16
*B:* 14

Gum, chewing
*B:* 33

**H**

Haish, Jacob
*A:* 114

Haiti
*B:* 165

Hall, G. Stanley
*B:* 36–37

Hall, Prescott
*A:* 82

Hall, Sharlot
*A:* 120

Halpin, Maria
*A:* 151

Hamilton, Alice
*B:* 200

Hampton Institute
*B:* 230

Hancock, Winfield
*A:* 15

Handy, Truman P.
*PS:* 157

Handy, W. C.
*A:* 230

Harding, Warren G.
*A:* 59

Harlan, John Marshall
*PS:* 100, 101–2, 102 (ill.), 105

"Harmony Club Waltz" (Joplin)
*B:* 106

Harper, Fletcher
*B:* 147

Harper, Joseph W., Jr.
*B:* 147

*Harper's Monthly* (publication)
*PS:* 108

*Harper's Weekly* (publication)
*A:* 5, 206–7
*B:* 143, 145, 147–48

**Harriman, Edward**
  *B:* 75 (ill.), **75–82**
  early years, *B:* 75–76
  expedition, *B:* 77–79
  Hill, James, *B:* 80
  legacy, *B:* 80–81
  Northern Securities
    Company, *B:* 157
  railroads, *B:* 76–77
  Roosevelt, Theodore, *B:* 161
Harriman Expedition
  *B:* 77–79
Harriman State Park
  *B:* 81
Harris, Isaac
  *PS:* 197, 207, 208
Harris, Richard T.
  *A:* 234–35
**Harrison, Benjamin**
  *B:* 83 (ill.), **83–92**
  anti-imperialism, *B:* 128
  domestic policy, *B:* 85–87
  early years, *B:* 83–84
  foreign policy, *B:* 87–90
  monetary policy, *A:* 129
  presidency overview,
    *A:* 157 (ill.), 157–60
  presidential election of 1888,
    *A:* 19 (ill.), 33; *B:* 20, 84–85
  presidential election of 1892,
    *A:* 142; *B:* 90–91
  Roosevelt, Theodore, *B:* 152
  tariffs, *A:* 18, 137, 138
Harrison, Benjamin (Colonel)
  *B:* 83
Harrison, William Henry
  *B:* 83
  *PS:* 31–32
Harvey, George
  *B:* 219
Hawaii
  *A:* 93, 159, 161, 165–67,
    166 (ill.)
  *B:* 89–90, 128–29
Hay, Mary Garrett
  *PS:* 81 (ill.)

Hayden, Belle
  *B:* 107
Hayes, Rutherford B.
  *A:* 10–13, 11 (ill.), 14, 50
  *B:* 84, 89, 120
Haymarket Square riot
  *A:* 51–53, 52 (ill.)
  *B:* 55, 63
Health
  *A:* 67–69, 70
Health, occupational. *See*
  Occupational health and safety
Heine, Heinrich
  *PS:* 24
Henri, Robert
  *A:* 217
Henry Street Settlement
  *B:* 5
Hepburn Act of 1906
  *A:* 263–64
  *B:* 161
Hepburn, William P.
  *A:* 263–64
  *B:* 161
Hetch-Hetchy
  *B:* 138
Hewett, Edgar Lee
  *PS:* 139–40, 142–44
Hill, James
  *B:* 80, 157
Hillman, Bessie Abramowitz
  *B:* 200
**Hine, Lewis**
  *A:* 189, 192
  *B:* 93 (ill.), **93–103**
  child-labor reform, *B:* 98
    (ill.), 99, 99 (ill.)
  early years, *B:* 94
  freelance and interpretive
    career, *B:* 99, 101
  later years, *B:* 102–3
  photographic documentaries,
    *B:* 94–96
  photographic legacy, *B:* 93–94
Hires Root Beer
  *B:* 248

*The History of the Standard Oil
  Company* (Tarbell)
  *A:* 207
  *PS:* 154–58
*The History of Woman Suffrage*
  (Anthony, Gage, and Stanton)
  *B:* 207, 209
Hobart, Garret A.
  *A:* 168
  *B:* 131
Home loans. *See* Mortgages
Home-building kits
  *PS:* 175–79, 193–95
Homeless people
  *B:* 100 (ill.)
Homelessness
  *PS:* 65 (ill.)
Homer, Winslow
  *A:* 215–16, 216 (ill.)
Homestead Strike of 1892
  *A:* 54–56
  *B:* 57–59
Hong Kong
  *A:* 274
*Honor Bilt Modern Homes* (catalog)
  *PS:* 177 (ill.)
Hoover, Herbert
  *B:* 8
Hoover, J. Edgar
  *B:* 63
Horizontal integration
  *A:* 32
Houdini, Harry
  *A:* 226 (ill.), 226–27
Housing. *See also* Tenements
  *PS:* 175–79, 193–95
  coal miners, *A:* 41
  immigrants, *A:* 74
  mail-order, *A:* 209
  Riis, Jacob, on, *A:* 186
*How the Other Half Lives* (Riis)
  *A:* 186
  *B:* 100
  *PS:* 63–71
Howe, Julia Ward
  *PS:* 74

HRRR (Hudson River Railroad)
  **B:** 224–25, 226 (ill.)
Hudson River Railroad (HRRR)
  **B:** 224–25, 226 (ill.)
Hudson River Steamboat
  Association
  **B:** 223
Hull-House
  **A:** 186
  **B:** 1, 3–7
Hunter, Robert
  **A:** 171, 172
Hunting
  **A:** 122, 123
  **B:** 158
  **PS:** 42 (ill.), 42–46, 49 (ill.)
Hunting rights
  **A:** 100, 101

**I**

ICC (Interstate Commerce
  Commission)
  **A:** 29–30, 155, 264, 271
  **B:** 161–62
Icebergs
  **PS:** 220, 221 (ill.), 223
Idaho
  **B:** 90
Ideal Novelty and Toy Company
  **B:** 160
Idealism
  **B:** 36
IFREMER (French Research
  Institute for Exploitation
  of the Sea)
  **PS:** 223
Illinois
  **A:** 56–57
  **B:** 195
Illinois Central Railroad
  **B:** 77, 80
Illinois Industrial School for Girls
  **B:** 199
Immigrants and immigration
  **B:** 95 (ill.)

Arthur, Chester A., **A:** 16
assistance for, **B:** 198
British, **A:** 90
Canadian, **A:** 90, 92
child labor, **PS:** 125, 126
Chinese, **A:** 76, 77–79, 78
  (ill.), 81 (ill.), 156–57, 157–
  58, 165; **B:** 14, 84, 127,
  147; **PS:** 1–10, 5 (ill.)
coal miners, **A:** 39–47
eugenics, **A:** 176
garment industry, **PS:** 197, 198
German, **A:** 86–88
Hine, Lewis, **B:** 94–96
housing, **PS:** 194
Hull-House, **B:** 1, 3–5
Irish, **A:** 39–43, 72–77
Italian, **A:** 88–90, 89 (ill.)
Japanese, **A:** 93
Jewish, **A:** 82–86
journey of, **A:** 66–70, 67 (ill.),
  72 (ill.)
Lazarus, Emma, **PS:** 23–27
meatpacking industry, **PS:** 173
Mexican, **A:** 92–93
naturalization, **A:** 79–82
notable, **A:** 91
population, **B:** 90
process, **A:** 70
railroad industry, **A:** 70–72
reasons for emigrating,
  **A:** 72–73
records, **A:** 65–66, 67
religion, **A:** 44–45
Scandinavian, **A:** 90
sources, **A:** 71
sweatshop employment, **A:** 53
tenements, **A:** 23, 24 (ill.)
urban areas, **A:** 93–98
Wald, Lillian, **B:** 4–5
westward migration,
  **A:** 114–16
working class, **PS:** 61–62, 163
Immigration Act of 1907
  **PS:** 27
Immigration Act of 1924
  **A:** 176

Immigration Restriction League
  (IRL)
  **A:** 82
*Imperator* (ship)
  **PS:** 225
Imperialism. *See* Expansionism;
  Territorial expansion
Impressionism
  **A:** 216–17
"In Roosevelt's Name We Bust
  Trusts: The Meat Inspection
  Act of 1906" (Junod)
  **PS:** 172
Incandescent lightbulbs
  **B:** 43, 47–48, 50–51
Income tax
  **B:** 121–22, 123
Independence movements
  Cuba, **B:** 23, 129–30,
    153–54, 165
  Philippines, **B:** 130
Independent Labor Party
  **A:** 10
Indian Affairs, U.S. Bureau of
  **A:** 104
Indian Emancipation Act of
  1887. *See* Dawes Severalty Act
Indian New Deal. *See* Indian
  Reorganization Act of 1934
Indian Reorganization Act of
  1934
  **PS:** 37–38
Indian Rights Association
  **A:** 102
Indians, American. *See* Native
  Americans
Industrial Workers of the World
  (IWW)
  **A:** 61
Industrialism
  **A:** 21
Industrialization. *See also* Mass
  production
  **B:** 175
  child labor, **PS:** 126
  Gilded Age, **A:** 21–37

reforms, *PS:* 207
robber barons, *PS:* 51
social classes, *PS:* 53, 61–62,
163
Social Gospel, *PS:* 54
social problems, *PS:* 63
working conditions, *PS:* 163
Infants. *See* Children and youth
Inflation
*A:* 7, 9
*The Innocents Abroad* (Twain)
*B:* 214
Institute for Government Research
*PS:* 38
Integration
horizontal, *A:* 32
vertical, *A:* 26, 30
Interior, U.S. Department of the
*B:* 164
*PS:* 142
International Convention for
Safety of Life at Sea
*PS:* 222
International Ice Patrol
*PS:* 223
International Ladies' Garment
Workers Union
*PS:* 199
International trade
*B:* 85, 130–31, 167
International Woman Suffrage
Alliance
*PS:* 75
Interstate commerce
*A:* 29
Interstate Commerce Act of 1887
*A:* 17, 29, 135, 154–55, 264
*B:* 18–19
Interstate Commerce
Commission (ICC)
*A:* 29–30, 155, 264, 271
*B:* 161–62
Inventions and inventors
Bell, Alexander Graham,
*A:* 248–49
biology and life sciences,
*A:* 254

Eastman, George, *A:* 251–52
Edison, Thomas, *A:* 250
Ford, Henry, *A:* 252–54
Marconi, Guglielmo, *A:* 251
Tesla, Nikola, *A:* 250–51
Wright brothers, *A:* 241–47,
248
Iola. *See* Wells-Barnett, Ida B.
IRL (Immigration Restriction
League)
*A:* 82
Ismay, Bruce
*PS:* 217
IWW (Industrial Workers of the
World)
*A:* 61

**J**

Jack London State Historical Park
*B:* 117
Jackson, Helen Hunt
*A:* 102 (ill.), 102–3
Jackson Hole
*PS:* 147
James, Frank
*A:* 117
James, Henry
*A:* 212
James, Jesse
*A:* 116–17
Japan
*A:* 268
*B:* 166–67
Jay Cooke & Company
*A:* 33
Jennings, O. B.
*PS:* 157
Jewish Denominational Congress
*B:* 196
Jewish Ladies Sewing Society
*B:* 193–94
Jews. *See also* Anti-Semitism;
Pogroms
*A:* 76, 82–86, 87
*PS:* 22–23, 24, 199

"The Jews of New York" (Riis)
*A:* 87
Jim Crow laws
*A:* 138–39
*PS:* 98, 103
"Jim Smiley and His Jumping
Frog" (Twain)
*B:* 213
John Chinaman
*B:* 147
John Muir National Historic Site
*B:* 136
John Muir Trail
*B:* 138
Johnson, Eldridge
*A:* 229
Johnson, Jack
*A:* 222 (ill.), 222–23
Johnson, Robert Underwood
*B:* 136
Johnson, Sophia. *See* Vanderbilt,
Sophia
Jones, Mary Harris. *See* Jones,
Mother
Jones, Mother
*A:* 61, 61 (ill.)
**Joplin, Scott**
*A:* 202, 230
*B:* 105 (ill.), **105–10**
early years, *B:* 105–6
opera, *B:* 107–8
ragtime compositions,
*B:* 106–7
Journalism. *See also* Muckrakers
and muckraking
*PS:* 153, 159
Judaism
*B:* 60, 194, 197
Juh
*B:* 188
July, Jim
*A:* 118
Juneau, Joseph
*A:* 234–35
*The Jungle* (Sinclair)
*A:* 213

**B:** 163, 173, 176–79, 177 (ill.)
**PS:** 164, 166–71, 173
Junod, Suzanne White
**PS:** 172
Juvenile courts
**B:** 195
**PS:** 218–19

# K

Katmai National Monument
**PS:** 146
Keating-Owen Child Labor Act
of 1916
**A:** 278
Keeler, Charles Augustus
**B:** 77
Kelley, Oliver Hudson
**A:** 9, 133
Kellogg, Arthur
**B:** 96
Kershner, Jacob
**B:** 54–55, 56
Kickbacks
**A:** 29
Kicking Bear
**A:** 108
**B:** 187
Kimbrough, Mary Craig
**B:** 181
Kinetograph
**B:** 50
Kinetophone
**B:** 50
Kinetoscope
**B:** 50
*King Coal* (Sinclair)
**A:** 213
**B:** 180
Kittredge, Charmian
**B:** 114
KKK (Ku Klux Klan)
**A:** 2, 140
Klondike
**A:** 235–37, 237 (ill.)

Klondike Kings
**A:** 240–41
Knickerbocker Trust
**B:** 163
Knights of Labor (KOL)
**A:** 48–49, 51, 52–53, 54,
57, 135
**B:** 71
Know-Nothing Party
**A:** 76
KOL (Knights of Labor)
**A:** 48–49, 51, 52–53, 54, 57
**B:** 71
Korea
**A:** 268
**B:** 166–67
Kowee (Native American chief)
**A:** 234
Ku Klux Klan (KKK)
**A:** 2, 140
Kushel, Frank
**PS:** 175

# L

La Follette Seaman's Bill of 1915
**A:** 278
Labor and Commerce, U.S.
Department of
**B:** 158
Labor movement. *See also* Child
labor; specific labor organizations
**PS:** 198–200, 205, 207
African Americans, **A:** 141
American Federation of
Labor, **A:** 53–54
Cleveland, Grover, **A:** 18,
161–63
coal mining, **A:** 39–48, 60,
62; **B:** 157–58
economic depression, **A:** 133
Great Railroad Strike, **A:** 49–51
Great Southwest Strike, **B:** 71
Harrison, Benjamin, **B:** 90
Hayes, Rutherford B., **A:** 11

Haymarket Square riot,
**A:** 51–53, 52 (ill.)
Homestead Strike of 1892,
**A:** 54–56; **B:** 57–59
Idaho miners' strike, **B:** 127
Jews, **A:** 85–86
Knights of Labor, **A:** 48–49, 51
Ludlow massacre, **A:** 62 (ill.),
62–63
McKinley, William, **A:** 165;
**B:** 120–21, 127
political parties, **A:** 8–10
Pullman strike, **A:** 56–57;
**B:** 21–22
reforms, **A:** 57, 188–93
Roosevelt, Theodore,
**A:** 260–61; **B:** 157–58
Wilson, Woodrow, **A:** 278
women, **A:** 179
Labor, U.S. Department of
**B:** 123
Labor violence
Great Southwest Strike, **B:** 71
Haymarket Square riot, **B:** 55
Pullman strike, **B:** 21
Laboratory schools
**B:** 37–39
Lacey Act of 1900
**A:** 123
Lacey, John F.
**A:** 123
**PS:** 140, 140 (ill.), 142
Lady Liberty. *See* Statue of Liberty
Laissez faire
**A:** 37, 57
Lake Chautauqua
**B:** 217
Lake Ontario Southern Railroad
**B:** 76
Lake Shore & Michigan Southern
Railroad
**B:** 225
Lakota
**A:** 108–10
**B:** 183–89
**PS:** 14–19

Lamps, electric
  *A:* 250
Lamps, incandescent. *See*
  Incandescent lightbulbs
Land grants
  *A:* 114–16
Land preservation
  *B:* 87, 159, 164
Land Revision Act of 1891
  *A:* 159
  *B:* 87
Land rights
  *A:* 100, 102–3, 105, 108, 155
  *B:* 19, 184–85, 189
  *PS:* 17–18, 31–39, 144
Landis, Kenesaw
  *B:* 31
*The Last of the Mohicans* (Cooper)
  *A:* 119
  *PS:* 34
Latin America
  *B:* 87–88
Lazarus, Emma
  *A:* 69
  *PS:* 21–29, 24 (ill.)
  anti-Semitism encountered,
    *PS:* 22–23
  Jewish identity, *PS:* 24
  "The New Colossus," *PS:* 23,
    25–26
  Statue of Liberty, *PS:* 21–22
League of Nations
  *A:* 279
League of Women Voters
  *PS:* 75
Lectures
  *B:* 216, 217
Lee, Alice Hathaway
  *B:* 152
Lefebvre de Laboulaye, Édouard-
  René
  *PS:* 21
Lehigh & Wilkes Barre Coal
  Company
  *A:* 44
Lehigh Railroad
  *A:* 44

Leidy, George
  *B:* 27
Leonard, Dutch
  *B:* 30–31
Leopold, Aldo
  *A:* 120
Leslie, Frank
  *B:* 142
  *PS:* 5 (ill.)
Leupp, Charles
  *B:* 66
Lewis, Meriwether
  *A:* 119
Liberty Island
  *A:* 69
Libraries
  *A:* 219, 220
Library of Congress
  *A:* 220
*LIFE* (publication)
  *PS:* 107, 108, 120
Lightbulbs
  *A:* 250
Lightbulbs, incandescent.
  *See* Incandescent lightbulbs
Lincoln, Abraham
  *A:* 42, 76
  *B:* 143, 237
Liquor abstinence. *See*
  Temperance movement
Liquor moderation movement.
  *See* Temperance movement
Literacy tests
  *A:* 82, 83
  *PS:* 27
Literature
  *A:* 118–21, 207–13
Little Bighorn, Battle of. *See*
  Battle of Little Bighorn
Littlefield, Henry
  *A:* 146–47
*Living My Life* (Goldman)
  *B:* 59
Livingston, Robert R.
  *B:* 222
Lloyd, Henry Demarest
  *A:* 33

Loans, home. *See* Mortgages
Loeb, Jacob
  *A:* 254
Log Cabin Presidents
  *A:* 19
**London, Jack**
  *A:* 211–12
  *B:* 111 (ill.), **111–17,**
    114 (ill.)
  Beauty Ranch, *B:* 115–16
  depression and declining
    health, *B:* 116
  early years, *B:* 111–12
  legacy, *B:* 117
  writing career, *B:* 112, 114–15
  writing style, *B:* 111, 115
Lost Presidents. *See* Arthur,
  Chester A.; Garfield, James A.;
  Harrison, Benjamin; Hayes,
  Rutherford B.
Louisiana
  *PS:* 98, 101
Ludlow massacre
  *A:* 62 (ill.), 62–63
Lutheranism
  *A:* 87–88
Lynching
  *A:* 140 (ill.), 140–41, 275
  *B:* 128, 237, 239, 240 (ill.),
    241–42, 243
  *PS:* 86, 88–89, 90 (ill.), 93
Lyndhurst
  *B:* 72

## M

Machinery
  *A:* 22
MacKenzie, J. U.
  *B:* 44
Maddern, Bess
  *B:* 114
Magazines
  *A:* 206–7, 214–15
Magazines, pulp
  *B:* 174

Mail-order business
   *A:* 208–9
   *PS:* 175–76, 177, 178, 193
*Maine* (battleship)
   *B:* 129, 153, 154
Manchuria
   *A:* 268
   *B:* 166–67
Manhattan Elevated Rail
   Company
   *B:* 70
Mann-Elkins Act of 1910
   *A:* 271
Manny, Frank
   *B:* 94
Mansions
   *B:* 214–15, 215 (ill.),
      227 (ill.), 228
Manufacturing. *See* Industrialization
"Maple Leaf Rag" (Joplin)
   *B:* 106, 107 (ill.)
Marconi, Guglielmo
   *A:* 251
Maritime safety
   *PS:* 222–23
Marketing
   *A:* 23, 116
Marriage
   *B:* 60
Marshall, Thurgood
   *PS:* 103, 105
Mass production
   *A:* 22
Mass transit
   *A:* 95–96
Massacre, Ludlow
   *A:* 62–63
Mato Wanahtaka. *See* Kicking
   Bear
May, Karl
   *A:* 120
Maytown (Sears Modern Home
   Number 167)
   *PS:* 184 (ill.)
McCabe, James D.
   *PS:* 63

McCarty, William Henry.
   *See* Billy the Kid
*McClure's Magazine*
   *A:* 35, 36, 206 (ill.), 207
McKinley Tariff of 1890
   *A:* 18, 137–38, 158, 159
   *B:* 85, 90, 120
**McKinley, William**
   *B:* 119 (ill.), **119–32,**
      126 (ill.)
   assassination, *B:* 60, 131–32
   conservation movement, *A:* 123
   Cuba, *A:* 161
   early years, *B:* 120
   Hawaii, *A:* 161; *B:* 90
   legacy, *B:* 119, 132
   Philippines, *A:* 266
   political life, *B:* 120–21
   presidency, *A:* 163–69, 164
      (ill.), 166 (ill.); *B:* 125–31
   presidential election of 1896,
      *A:* 35, 145; *B:* 23, 121–25
   presidential election of 1900,
      *A:* 145–46
   Roosevelt, Theodore, *A:* 258;
      *B:* 155
   Spanish-American War,
      *A:* 18–19; *B:* 153–54
   tariffs, *A:* 137, 158; *B:* 85
McParland, James
   *A:* 45–47, 48
Meat Inspection Act of 1906
   *A:* 213, 264
   *B:* 178, 180 (ill.)
   *PS:* 172
Meatpacking industry
   *B:* 100, 157, 162 (ill.),
      162–63, 176–78, 180 (ill.)
   *PS:* 169 (ill.)
   Armour, Philip, *PS:* 166
   Sinclair, Upton, *PS:* 164,
      166–73
   Swift, Gustavus, *PS:* 165
Media
   *A:* 168
Mediation
   *B:* 157–58

*Memphis Free Speech and
   Headlight* (newspaper)
   *B:* 239
Memphis, Tennessee
   *B:* 239
*Men at Work* (Hine)
   *B:* 101
Menlo Park, New Jersey
   *B:* 46
Mergers and acquisitions. *See also*
   Horizontal integration
   *A:* 32
Merriam, C. Hart
   *B:* 78
Merriam, Lewis
   *PS:* 38
Merriam Report
   *PS:* 38
Metalworking industry
   *A:* 23
*The Metropolis* (Sinclair)
   *B:* 180
Metropolitan Life Insurance
   Company
   *B:* 5
Mexico
   *A:* 272–73
   *B:* 188–89
Michtom, Morris
   *B:* 160
Microsoft Corporation
   *A:* 34
   *PS:* 160
Military draft
   *A:* 42
   *B:* 62
Miller, Helen Day
   *B:* 67
Miller, Lewis
   *B:* 217
Milwaukee, Wisconsin
   *A:* 88
*Miner's Journal* (publication)
   *A:* 42–43
Mining, coal. *See* Coal mining
Minstrel shows
   *A:* 138, 139 (ill.), 225–26

Miscegenation
    *A:* 222–24
Missouri
    *B:* 212
Mitchell, John
    *A:* 60
Mitchell, John Ames
    *PS:* 108, 120
Mitchell, Silas Weir
    *B:* 178–79
Moderation movement. *See*
    Temperance movement
Mollies. *See* Molly Maguires
Molly Maguires
    *A:* 43, 46
Monetary policy. *See also* Silver
    Bryan, William Jennings,
        *A:* 143–44, 163
    Cleveland, Grover, *A:* 143, 160
    economic depression,
        *A:* 127–29
    Gilded Age, *A:* 7
    Greenback Party, *A:* 9, 135
    Hayes, Rutherford B., *A:* 11–12
    McKinley, William, *A:* 163
    Populist Party, *A:* 143
Monopolies. *See also* Horizontal
    integration; Trusts and trust-
    busting; Vertical integration
    *A:* 18, 33–34, 158, 260
    *B:* 32, 86, 157, 222–23
    *PS:* 152, 153
Montana
    *B:* 90
Montgomery Ward
    *A:* 208
    *PS:* 176
Monuments, national. *See*
    National parks and monuments
Morgan, J. P.
    *A:* 35, 62, 160–61, 264–65
    *B:* 21, 80, 157, 161, 163
    *PS:* 52, 56, 159 (ill.)
Morris, George Sylvester
    *B:* 36
Morris, William
    *A:* 219

Mortgages
    *PS:* 176, 193
Morton, Julius S.
    *A:* 121
*Mother Earth* (publication)
    *B:* 60, 61–62
Mother Jones. *See* Jones, Mother
Motherhood
    *PS:* 78–80
*Mothers in Bondage* (Sanger)
    *A:* 175
Motion pictures
    *A:* 227–28
Mott, James
    *B:* 205
Mott, Lucretia
    *B:* 204, 205
Movies. *See* Motion pictures
Muckrakers and muckraking
    *A:* 35–36, 186, 207, 213,
        259–60
    *B:* 100, 156, 173
    *PS:* 153, 164, 167
Mugwumps
    *A:* 8, 8 (ill.), 17
**Muir, John**
    *A:* 120, 121, 122 (ill.)
    *B:* 133 (ill.), **133–40,**
        137 (ill.)
    California years, *B:* 134–35
    early years, *B:* 133–34
    Harriman, Edward,
        *B:* 77, 81
    Hetch-Hetchy battle, *B:* 138
    later years, *B:* 138–39
    legacy, *B:* 139
    Roosevelt, Theodore,
        *B:* 159
    Sierra Club, *B:* 136–37
    Yosemite National Park,
        *B:* 136
Mulrooney, Belinda
    *A:* 241
Music. *See also* Ragtime music
    *A:* 228–30
    *B:* 248

NAACP (National Association for
    the Advancement of Colored
    People)
    *A:* 141, 180
    *B:* 7, 243
    *PS:* 103
NACW (National Association of
    Colored Women)
    *A:* 180
**Nast, Thomas**
    *A:* 4 (ill.), 5, 206–7,
        211 (ill.)
    *B:* 141 (ill.), **141–49,**
        145 (ill.), 146 (ill.), 147 (ill.)
    early years, *B:* 141–42
    *Harper's Weekly,* *B:* 143
    legacy, *B:* 148
    popularity wanes,
        *B:* 146–48
    Tweed, William Marcy
        "Boss," *B:* 143
*Nast's Weekly* (publication)
    *B:* 148
National Afro-American Council
    *A:* 141
    *B:* 241
National American Woman
    Suffrage Association (NAWSA)
    *A:* 182, 187
    *B:* 7, 207
    *PS:* 75, 76
National Association for the
    Advancement of Colored
    People (NAACP)
    *A:* 141, 180
    *B:* 7, 243
    *PS:* 103
National Association of Colored
    Women (NACW)
    *A:* 180
National Audubon Society
    *A:* 122
National Birth Control League
    *A:* 175

National Child Labor Committee
(NCLC)
*A:* 193
*B:* 96, 99
*PS:* 135
*National Citizen and Ballot Box*
(newspaper)
*B:* 208
National Committee on the
Cause and Cure of War
*PS:* 75
National Conference of Charities
and Corrections
*B:* 7
National Council of Jewish
Women (NCJW)
*A:* 83
*B:* 193, 196–98, 199–200
National Council of Women of
the United States
*PS:* 76–77
National Farmers' Alliance
*A:* 133, 138
National Forest Service
*A:* 123, 268, 269, 270
*B:* 164
National Indian Defense Association
*A:* 102
National Negro Business League
*B:* 234
National parks and monuments
*A:* 121, 122, 123
*B:* 136
*PS:* 140, 141, 142, 146, 148
National Phonograph Company
*B:* 49
National Reclamation Act of 1902
*A:* 262
*PS:* 48
National Tuberculosis Commission
*B:* 99
National Union Labor Party. *See*
Union Labor Party (ULP)
National Woman Suffrage
Association (NWSA)
*A:* 182

*B:* 206–7, 208–9
*PS:* 74, 76
National Woman's Christian
Temperance Union (WCTU)
*A:* 145
Native Americans
agriculture, *A:* 120–21
artifacts, *PS:* 139
assimilation, *PS:* 17–18,
32–33, 33 (ill.), 37
Cleveland, Grover, *A:* 157;
*B:* 20
Dawes Severalty Act, *A:* 17,
155; *B:* 19; *PS:* 31–39
Geronimo, *B:* 188–89
literature, *A:* 118
national monuments, *PS:* 144
Roosevelt, Theodore, *PS:* 43
Sitting Bull, *B:* 183–91;
*PS:* 13–19
treaties, *PS:* 14
westward expansion,
*A:* 99–105, 108–11
Nativism
*A:* 76
*PS:* 27
Naturalization Act of 1870
*A:* 80
*PS:* 3
Nature
*A:* 120–24
Naval Consulting Board
*B:* 50
Navy, U.S.
*B:* 87
NAWSA (National American
Woman Suffrage Association)
*A:* 182, 187
*B:* 207
*PS:* 75, 76
NCJW (National Council of
Jewish Women). *See* National
Council of Jewish Women
(NCJW)
NCLC (National Child Labor
Committee)
*A:* 193

*B:* 96, 99
*PS:* 135
Negro Fellowship Reading Room
and Social Center
*B:* 242
Negroes. *See* African Americans
Neighborhood Playhouse
*B:* 5
Nesbit, Evelyn
*PS:* 110 (ill.), 110–11, 113 (ill.)
*The Netmenders* (Homer)
*A:* 216 (ill.)
"The New Colossus" (Lazarus)
*PS:* 22, 23, 25–27, 26 (ill.)
New Deal
*A:* 59
New Haven Railroad
*B:* 163
New Mexico
*PS:* 140
New York
*A:* 150–51
*B:* 11–12, 208–9
New York & Erie Railroad.
*See* Erie Railroad
New York & Harlem Railroad
(NY & H)
*B:* 224
New York Central Railroad
(NYC)
*B:* 67, 225, 226, 226 (ill.)
New York City
fire safety, *PS:* 207
immigrant population, *PS:* 27
Jews, *A:* 83–85, 87
patronage, *A:* 4–5, 76
Riis, Jacob, on, *PS:* 62–71, 65
(ill.)
tenements, *A:* 183–85, 184 (ill.)
Tweed, William Marcy
"Boss," *B:* 67–68, 143–45
Wald, Lillian, *B:* 4–5
New York Customs House
*B:* 14
*New York Illustrated News*
*B:* 143

New York Woman Suffrage
  Association
  *B:* 208
*New York World* (newspaper)
  *B:* 70
Newark Telegraph Works
  *B:* 45
Newfoundland
  *B:* 19–20
Newlands Act of 1902
  *B:* 159
Newman, Pauline
  *PS:* 198
Newsies
  *A:* 188–89
  *PS:* 127
Newspapers
  *A:* 213–15
Nickelodeons
  *A:* 227
Nickels
  *PS:* 18, 18 (ill.)
1920s
  *A:* 279–80
Nineteenth Amendment. *See also*
  Women's suffrage movement
  *A:* 278
  *B:* 203, 208, 250
  *PS:* 80, 81 (ill.)
Niota (Sears Modern Home
  Number 161)
  *PS:* 183 (ill.)
No-Conscription League
  *B:* 62
Nobel Peace Prizes
  *B:* 8, 167
Noble Order of the Knights of
  Labor. *See* Knights of Labor
  (KOL)
North American Construction
  Company
  *PS:* 176
North Dakota
  *B:* 90
North Pole
  *A:* 254

Northern Indiana Railroad
  *B:* 225
Northern Pacific Railroad
  *B:* 80
*Northern Securities Co. v.
  United States*
  *B:* 80
Northern Securities Company
  *A:* 260
  *B:* 80, 157
Northwest Territory
  *A:* 100
"Not Worrying about Her
  Rights" (artwork)
  *PS:* 118 (ill.)
Novels
  *A:* 119, 211–12
  dime, *B:* 174
Nursing care
  *B:* 4–5
NWSA (National Woman
  Suffrage Association)
  *A:* 182
  *B:* 206–7, 208–9
  *PS:* 74, 76
NY & H (New York & Harlem
  Railroad)
  *B:* 224
NYC (New York Central
  Railroad). *See* New York
  Central Railroad (NYC)

Occupational health and safety
  *A:* 41
  coal mining, *PS:* 127–28
  garment industry, *PS:* 197,
    198, 200, 205–7
  meatpacking, *PS:* 167
O'Donnell, Hugh
  *A:* 55
  *B:* 58, 59
Ogdensburg & Lake Champlain
  Railroad Company
  *B:* 76

*Oil* (Sinclair)
  *B:* 180
Oil industry. *See* Petroleum
  industry
Open Door policy
  *B:* 130–31, 167
Opera
  *B:* 107–8
Opiates
  *A:* 210
Oral tradition
  *A:* 118–19
Order of Patrons of Husbandry.
  *See* Grange
Organization of American States
  *B:* 89
"Original Rags" (Joplin)
  *B:* 106
Osborn (Sears Modern Home
  Number 12050)
  *PS:* 188 (ill.)
*Our National Parks* (Muir)
  *B:* 137
Outfitters
  *A:* 235–36, 238
Outlaws
  *A:* 116–18

Pacific Mail Steamship Company
  *B:* 81
Pacifism. *See* Antiwar movement
Packer, Asa
  *A:* 43–45, 46, 48
Pajarito Plateau
  *PS:* 140, 142
Panama
  *B:* 165–66
Panama Canal
  *A:* 265–67, 267 (ill.)
  *B:* 165–66
Pan-American Conference
  *B:* 88
Pan-American Union
  *A:* 159

Pan-Americanism
  *B:* 87–88
Panic of 1907
  *A:* 264–65
  *B:* 163–64
Paper currency
  *B:* 121
Paris Peace Treaty of 1898
  *A:* 167
  *B:* 130
Park, Maud Wood
  *PS:* 81 (ill.)
Parker, Alton B.
  *A:* 263
  *B:* 161
Parks, national. *See* National
  parks and monuments
Parrish, Charles
  *A:* 44–45, 46, 48
Parrish, Maxfield
  *PS:* 108
Parthenogenesis
  *A:* 254
Parties, political. *See* Political
  parties
Patronage
  *B:* 13–16
  Arthur, Chester A., *A:* 16
  Cleveland, Grover, *A:* 153,
    154 (ill.)
  Conkling, Roscoe, *A:* 14
  Garfield, James A., *A:* 15–16
  Hayes, Rutherford B., *A:* 11
  Irish immigrants, *A:* 75–76
  Mugwumps, *A:* 8
  reform, *A:* 7
  Tammany Hall, *A:* 4–5
Patrons of Husbandry. *See*
  Grange
Pattison, Robert
  *B:* 58
Payne-Aldrich Tariff
  *A:* 272
Payne, Sereno
  *A:* 272
Peace negotiations
  *A:* 268, 278–79

Peary, Robert
  *A:* 254
Peck and Snyder
  *B:* 32
Pendleton Act of 1883
  *A:* 16
  *B:* 14–15
Pennsylvania
  Homestead Strike, *A:* 54–56
  labor movement, *A:* 39, 41,
    42 (ill.), 43–44, 45, 48
Pennsylvania Railroad
  Great Railroad Strike,
    *A:* 49–51, 50 (ill.)
  Harriman, Edward, *B:* 76
Pension Bureau, U.S.
  *B:* 17–18
Pensions
  *A:* 17, 153–54
People's Party. *See* Populist Party
Petrified Forest
  *PS:* 145, 146
Petroleum industry
  *A:* 26–27, 32–33
  *PS:* 152, 154–58, 160
Philadelphia Athletics
  *B:* 31
Philanthropy
  *A:* 31, 87, 171–72, 219
  *B:* 195, 197, 226–27
  Armour, Philip, *PS:* 166
  Carnegie, Andrew,
    *PS:* 52–53, 54–57, 58
  Morgan, J. P., *PS:* 56
  poverty, *PS:* 63
  Rockefeller, John D.,
    *PS:* 56–57, 160
Philippines
  *A:* 19, 167, 266, 268
  *B:* 130, 164, 167, 216
Philosophy, educational. *See*
  Educational philosophy
Phonographs
  *A:* 229
  *B:* 47, 48–49, 50
Photography
  *A:* 217–18

  *B:* 93–103
  *PS:* 62–63, 68–69
Picasso, Pablo
  *A:* 217
Pickford, Mary
  *A:* 178, 178 (ill.)
"A Picture of Her Face" (Joplin)
  *B:* 106
"Picturesque America—Anywhere
  along the Coast" (artwork)
  *PS:* 116 (ill.)
Pilz, George
  *A:* 234
Pinchot, Gifford
  *A:* 123, 124, 268–69, 270,
    270 (ill.), 272
  *B:* 159, 164
Pinkerton, Allan
  *A:* 46–47
Pinkerton National Detective
  Agency
  *A:* 45–47, 47 (ill.), 55
  *B:* 58
Pinkerton, Robert II
  *A:* 47
Pittsburgh, Pennsylvania
  *B:* 96
Plains Indian Wars
  *A:* 100–101
  *B:* 184, 186
  *PS:* 13–18, 32, 47
Planes (aircraft). *See* Aircraft
Planned Parenthood Federation
  of America
  *A:* 175
Platt Amendment of 1903
  *B:* 165
Platt, Ida
  *B:* 200
"Please Say You Will" (Joplin)
  *B:* 106
Plessy, Homer
  *A:* 139
  *PS:* 98, 102
*Plessy v. Ferguson*
  *A:* 139
  *PS:* 97–106

circumstances of, *PS:* 97–98, 100

excerpts, *PS:* 100–102

legacy, *PS:* 102–3, 105

Poetry
A: 120

Pogroms
*PS:* 24

Political cartoons
A: 206–7

Political ethics. *See also* Corruption in government
A: 4–5

Political machines. *See* Patronage

Political parties. *See also* names of specific parties
farmer and labor, A: 8–10, 133–36

Pooling
B: 18, 19

Pools
A: 70, 155

Pope, Edison and Co.
B: 45

Pope, Franklin L.
B: 44–45

Popular votes. *See* Presidential elections

Population
A: 93–94

Populism
African Americans, A: 141–42

growth, A: 133, 138

presidential election of 1892, A: 142–43

in *Wizard of Oz*, A: 146–47

Populist Party
A: 138, 142–45, 159, 163

B: 121–25

Potato Famine
A: 73

Potter, J. A.
B: 58

Poverty
in class distinction, *PS:* 211–12

Riis, Jacob, on, *PS:* 62–71, 68 (ill.), 69 (ill.)

*Poverty* (Hunter)
A: 171, 172

Powderly, Terence V.
A: 51, 53

B: 71

Pragmatism
A: 194

B: 35

Prairies
A: 90, 92

Pratt, Zadock
B: 66

Prejudice. *See also* Anti-Semitism; Nativism
immigrant, *PS:* 3, 4, 5 (ill.), 6, 23, 25, 26, 27

Native American, *PS:* 17, 33–34

Presidential elections
1876, A: 10–11; B: 89

1880, A: 9, 13–15, 15 (ill.); B: 15 (ill.), 89

1884, A: 8 (ill.), 9, 16–17, 149–51, 152 (ill.), 153; B: 12–13, 15, 89

1888, A: 18, 33, 135, 137, 157–58; B: 20, 84–85, 89, 152

1892, A: 18, 138, 142–43, 160; B: 20, 89, 90–91

1896, A: 18–19, 35, 143–45, 162–63; B: 23, 121–25

1900, A: 168, 258; B: 131, 155

1904, A: 262–63; B: 159–61

1908, A: 269–70; B: 168

1912, A: 275–76, 277 (ill.); B: 168–70

2000, A: 12–13

Presidential power. *See also* Veto power
B: 85, 87

*PS:* 145–47, 148

*Presidential Problems* (Cleveland)
B: 23

Price, Hiram
A: 101

Primary elections
A: 276

B: 168–69

Prizefighting. *See* Boxing

Progressive education movement
B: 40

Progressive Era
advertising, A: 204–5, 206–7

architecture, A: 218

education reform, A: 193–96

gold prospecting, A: 234–35, 237 (ill.), 239–41, 240 (ill.)

government assistance during, A: 196–97

inventions, A: 248–54

labor reform, A: 188–93

legacy, A: 279

literature, A: 207–13

motion pictures, A: 227–28

music, A: 228–30

1920s vs., A: 279–80

Roosevelt, Theodore, A: 257–69

settlement houses, A: 185–88

social classes, A: 171–72

Taft, William Howard, A: 270–76

urban reform, A: 182–85

Wilson, Woodrow, A: 276–79

women, A: 174–75, 177–82

Progressive Party
A: 276–77

B: 169, 170

Prohibition
A: 145, 181, 279

B: 248, 249

Propaganda
B: 248

Prospecting, gold
A: 77, 234–35, 237 (ill.), 239–41, 240 (ill.)

*PS:* 1

Prostitutes
A: 79, 80

Protected land
*PS:* 139–48

Protective tariffs. *See* Tariffs

Protestantism
 *A:* 40, 45, 75

Public assistance. *See* Government
 assistance

Public Beach Campaign
 (Chicago, Illinois)
 *B:* 199

Public health
 *PS:* 70, 71

Public speaking
 *A:* 158

*Puck* (publication)
 *PS:* 172

Puerto Rico
 *A:* 19, 167
 *B:* 164, 165

Pullman, George
 *A:* 56–57

Pullman Palace Car Company
 *A:* 56–57, 162
 *B:* 21–22

Pullman strike
 *A:* 56–57, 162, 162 (ill.)
 *B:* 21–22, 22 (ill.), 23

Pulp magazines
 *A:* 214–15
 *B:* 174

Pure Food and Drug Act of 1906
 *A:* 205, 213, 264
 *B:* 162, 163, 177
 *PS:* 166, 171

**Q**

Quakers
 *B:* 205

"The Question Mark" (artwork)
 *PS:* 110, 113 (ill.)

**R**

Race relations
 *B:* 128
 *PS:* 99, 100–102

Racial violence. *See also* Lynching
 *A:* 2, 140–41, 142, 275

Racism
 *A:* 203, 226, 227
 Columbian Exposition,
  *PS:* 85–94

Radio
 *A:* 250–51

*Rag Time Dance* (Joplin)
 *B:* 107

Ragtime music
 *A:* 228–29
 *B:* 105–9

Railroads and railroad industry
 agriculture, *A:* 133–34, 134 (ill.)
 antitrust actions, *B:* 157
 bankruptcies, *B:* 20
 big business, *A:* 28
 Chinese immigrants, *A:* 78,
  78 (ill.); *PS:* 2
 Cleveland, Grover, *A:* 17,
  154–55
 coal mining vs., *A:* 43–48
 Cody, Buffalo Bill, *A:* 106
 corruption, *A:* 29–30
 Gould, Jay, *B:* 67–69,
  70 (ill.), 71
 Harriman, Edward,
  *B:* 76–77, 79–80
 immigrants, *A:* 70–72
 industrialization, *A:* 21, 22
 investment, *A:* 130
 labor unions, *A:* 58
 Native American impact,
  *PS:* 13
 Populists, *B:* 121
 Pullman strike, *A:* 56–57, 162
 rate discrimination by, *B:* 18–19
 rebates, *A:* 32, 262; *B:* 18,
  19, 158
 regulation, *B:* 161–62
 robber barons, *A:* 26, 27
 Rockefeller, John D.,
  *PS:* 153–54, 155–58
 segregation, *PS:* 98
 Vanderbilt, Cornelius,
  *B:* 224–26, 226 (ill.)

 westward expansion, *A:* 111,
  113 (ill.), 113–16

*Ramona* (Jackson)
 *A:* 103

*Ranch Life and the Hunting-Trail*
 (Roosevelt)
 *PS:* 42–46

Ranches
 *PS:* 46

Raper, Arthur
 *PS:* 93

Rate discrimination
 *B:* 18–19, 158

Rauschenbusch, Walter
 *A:* 219

Reading Railroad
 *A:* 43

"The Reason Why the Colored
 American Is Not Represented
 in the World's Columbian
 Exposition" (Wells-Barnett)
 *B:* 241

Rebates and refunds
 *A:* 32, 155, 262
 *B:* 18, 19, 158
 *PS:* 153–54, 156–58

Reclamation Act of 1902. *See*
 Newlands Act of 1902

Reconstruction Era
 *A:* 1

Red Cross
 *B:* 99

*A Red Record: Tabulated Statistics
 and Alleged Causes of Lynchings
 in the United States, 1892–
 1893–1894* (Wells-Barnett)
 *B:* 242

Reed, Thomas B.
 *B:* 91

Reform, government. *See*
 Government reform

Reform Judaism. *See* Judaism

Refrigeration
 *PS:* 165

Refunds. *See* Rebates and
 refunds

Regulation, government.
 *See* Government regulation
Relativity
 *A:* 254
Religion
 *B:* 60, 248
 *PS:* 54
 German immigrants, *A:* 87–88
 interdenominational conflict,
  *A:* 44–45, 75
 Native American, *A:* 104,
  108–9
 political party affiliation,
  *A:* 6, 7
 Social Gospel movement,
  *A:* 219
Religious Society of Friends. *See*
 Quakers
Relocation of Native Americans
 *A:* 100
Remington, Frederic
 *PS:* 44, 44 (ill.)
Rensselaer & Saratoga Railroad
 *B:* 67
Republican Party
 Arthur, Chester A., *B:* 15
 Blaine, James G., *B:* 13–14
 elephant symbol, *B:* 147
 Gilded Age, *A:* 2–7
 Harrison, Benjamin, *A:* 159;
  *B:* 84
 McKinley, William, *A:* 165;
  *B:* 128
 Mugwumps, *A:* 8
 Populist Party, *A:* 142
 presidential election of 1876,
  *A:* 10–11
 presidential election of 1880,
  *A:* 13–1
 presidential election of 1888,
  *A:* 18
 presidential election of 1896,
  *B:* 125
 presidential election of 1900,
  *A:* 168
 presidential election of 1912,
  *A:* 276–77; *B:* 169

Roosevelt, Theodore,
 *A:* 262–63; *B:* 159–60
 tariffs, *A:* 136–38
Reservations, Native Americans.
 *See also* Native Americans
 *B:* 187
Resumption Act of 1875
 *A:* 11–12
Retaliation Act of 1887
 *A:* 156
 *B:* 20
Rice, Thomas (Daddy)
 *A:* 138
Rich, Sarah
 *B:* 96
Richardson, Henry H.
 *A:* 218
Right to vote for women. *See*
 Women's suffrage movement
Rights, civil. *See* Civil rights
Rights, fishing. *See* Fishing rights
Rights, hunting. *See* Hunting rights
Rights, land. *See* Land rights
Rights, women's. *See* Women's
 rights movement
Riis, Jacob
 *A:* 87, 186, 186 (ill.)
 *B:* 99, 100
 *PS:* 61–72, 62 (ill.)
Riots
 *A:* 42–43, 50, 57
Roaring Twenties
 *PS:* 120–21
Robber barons
 *A:* 26–28, 27 (ill.)
 *B:* 221
 *PS:* 51–53, 54, 56–57, 151–52
Roberts, Peter
 *PS:* 125–37
Robertson, William H.
 *B:* 14
Robinson, Bill (Bojangles)
 *A:* 227
Rockefeller, John D.
 *B:* 157, 226
 *PS:* 152 (ill.)
 industrialization, *A:* 24

labor movement, *A:* 63
philanthropy of, *A:* 196, 219
robber baron, *A:* 26–27;
 *PS:* 52, 54, 56–57, 159 (ill.)
Standard Oil empire,
 *A:* 32–37, 33 (ill.)
Tarbell, Ida M., *A:* 207;
 *PS:* 152–60
Rockefeller, John D., Jr.
 *A:* 63
Rockwell, Norman
 *PS:* 108
Roebuck, A. C.
 *A:* 208–9
Roman Catholicism
 *A:* 39, 40, 44–45, 75, 76
Roosevelt, Alice
 *B:* 152
Roosevelt, Franklin D.
 *A:* 59
 *B:* 102–3
 *PS:* 147
Roosevelt, Quentin
 *B:* 170
**Roosevelt, Theodore**
 *B:* 151 (ill.), **151–71,**
  153 (ill.), 160 (ill.),
  162 (ill.), 169 (ill.)
 *PS:* 42 (ill.), 49 (ill.)
 Addams, Jane, *B:* 8
 American West, *PS:* 42, 46–47
 antitrust actions, *B:* 86, 156–57
 Big Stick diplomacy, *B:* 158
 Chautauqua movement, *B:* 217
 conservation movement,
  *A:* 122 (ill.), 123–24, 270;
  *B:* 158–59; *PS:* 47–48, 140,
  144
 domestic policy, *B:* 161–64
 early years, *B:* 151–52
 food safety, *PS:* 170, 171
 foreign policy, *B:* 164–67
 labor arbitration by, *A:* 60, 62
 labor movement, *B:* 157–58
 later years, *B:* 170
 muckraking, *A:* 35–36; *PS:* 164
 Muir, John, *B:* 137

political beginnings, *B:* 152–53
presidency, *A:* 257–69,
    261 (ill.), 263, 267 (ill.);
    *B:* 155–56
presidential election of 1900,
    *A:* 168; *B:* 131
presidential election of 1904,
    *B:* 159–61
presidential election of 1912,
    *A:* 276, 277 (ill.); *B:* 168–70
Progressive Era, *A:* 19
*Ranch Life and the Hunting-
    Trail* excerpt, *PS:* 41–50
Riis, Jacob, *A:* 186; *B:* 100;
    *PS:* 70
robber barons, *PS:* 159 (ill.)
Sinclair, Upton, *B:* 176, 177
Spanish-American War,
    *B:* 153–55
Twain, Mark, *B:* 218
U.S. Steel, *A:* 272
Wald, Lillian, *B:* 5
Washington, Booker T.,
    *B:* 234, 234 (ill.)
Wilson, Woodrow, vs., *A:* 277
Rose, Pete
    *B:* 31
Rough Riders
    *A:* 257–58, 259 (ill.)
    *B:* 154–55
*Roughing It* (Twain)
    *B:* 214
    *PS:* 4
Russell, Charles Edward
    *A:* 264
    *B:* 163
Russia
    *A:* 268
    *B:* 166–67
    *PS:* 199
Russo-Japanese War
    *A:* 268
    *B:* 166–67
Ruth, Babe
    *B:* 31
Rutland & Washington Railroad
    *B:* 67

Sacagawea
    *A:* 119
Sacco, Nicola
    *A:* 213
    *B:* 181
Safaris
    *B:* 168, 169 (ill.)
Safety, maritime. *See* Maritime
    safety
Safety, occupational. *See*
    Occupational health and safety
Sage, Russell
    *A:* 27
Saint Joseph Railroad
    *B:* 80
Salisbury, Nate
    *A:* 106
Saloons
    *B:* 247
Salvage operations
    *PS:* 223–24
San Francisco, California
    *B:* 138
    *PS:* 1–12
San Francisco Earthquake of 1906
    *B:* 112, 113, 113 (ill.)
Sanger, Margaret
    *A:* 174 (ill.), 174–75, 176
Sanitation
    *A:* 97
Santa Claus
    *B:* 147, 147 (ill.)
Santee Rebellion
    *B:* 184
Sargent, John Singer
    *A:* 217
Sawyer, William
    *B:* 48
Saxton, Ida
    *B:* 120
Scalawags
    *A:* 3
Schoolchildren's Blizzard
    *A:* 92

Schools, experimental. *See also*
    Education
    *A:* 194
Scientific method
    *B:* 37
Scopes, John T.
    *B:* 123
Scopes Trial
    *B:* 123
Scott Act of 1888
    *A:* 81
    *PS:* 10
Scott, Caroline
    *B:* 84
Scott Joplin Opera Company
    *B:* 107
Scott, William
    *A:* 81
    *PS:* 10
Sears Modern Homes, 175–79,
    193–95
    Brentwood (Modern Home
        Numbers 13394C and
        13394D), *PS:* 190 (ill.)
    catalog cover, *PS:* 177 (ill.)
    Cedars (Modern Home
        Number C3278),
        *PS:* 189 (ill.)
    Chelsea (Modern Home
        Number 111), *PS:* 180 (ill.)
    Crafton (Modern Home
        Number 3318), *PS:* 192 (ill.)
    Croydon (Modern Home
        Number 13718),
        *PS:* 191 (ill.)
    Elsmore (Modern Home
        Numbers 208 and 2013),
        *PS:* 187 (ill.)
    Maytown (Modern Home
        Number 167), *PS:* 184 (ill.)
    Modern Home Number 52,
        *PS:* 188 (ill.)
    Modern Home Number 157,
        *PS:* 182 (ill.)
    Modern Home Number 191,
        *PS:* 185 (ill.)

Niota (Modern Home Number 161), **PS:** 183 (ill.)
Osborn (Modern Home Number 12050), **PS:** 188 (ill.)
Wabash/"Uncle Sam's Idea" (Modern Home Numbers 248 and 2003), **PS:** 186 (ill.)
Sears, Richard W.
    **A:** 208, 209
    **PS:** 175, 176 (ill.)
Sears, Roebuck and Co.
    **A:** 206, 208–9
    **PS:** 175–95
Seaver, Tom
    **B:** 31
*The Sea-Wolf* (London)
    **B:** 115
Secret organizations
    **A:** 43, 75
Segregation
    **A:** 139
    **B:** 238, 239, 242
    **PS:** 81, 97–103
Senators
    **B:** 121, 122
Seneca Falls Convention
    **B:** 205–6
Sensationalism
    **B:** 115
"Separate but equal" doctrine
    **A:** 139
    **B:** 239
    **PS:** 97, 101, 102, 103
Service, civil. *See* Civil service
Service, Robert
    **A:** 236
Settlement houses
    **A:** 185–88
    **B:** 1, 3–7
    **PS:** 70–71
Seventeenth Amendment
    **A:** 271
Sewing machines
    **A:** 30, 32
Sexes
    **PS:** 112 (ill.), 114 (ill.), 115 (ill.)

Sharecropping
    **A:** 3
Shaw, George Bernard
    **B:** 176
*A Sheaf of Leaves* (Solomon)
    **B:** 199
Shelton Loom Series
    **B:** 101
Sherman Antitrust Act of 1890
    **A:** 18, 34–35, 158, 260
    **B:** 86, 156–57
    **PS:** 153
Sherman, John
    **A:** 129, 158, 166 (ill.)
    **B:** 21, 86, 87 (ill.)
Sherman Silver Purchase Act
    **A:** 129, 129 (ill.), 158, 160
    **B:** 21, 86–87
Ships. *See also* names of specific ships
    **PS:** 222–23
Shirtwaist industry. *See* Garment industry
Short selling
    **B:** 224
Sierra Club
    **A:** 121–22
    **B:** 133, 136–37, 138, 139
Sierra Nevada
    **B:** 133, 134, 136–37
Silver
    **A:** 127–29, 143–44, 147, 158–59, 160
    Cleveland, Grover, **B:** 21
    Populist Party, **B:** 121, 122, 124
    Sherman Silver Purchase Act, **B:** 86–87
**Sinclair, Upton**
    **A:** 186, 213, 260, 264
    **B:** 173 (ill.), **173–82**
    **PS:** 163–74, 167 (ill.)
    early years, **B:** 156, 173–74
    *The Jungle*, **B:** 163, 173, 176–79, 177 (ill.)
    later works, **B:** 180–81
    socialism, **B:** 174–76, 178, 179

Siney, John
    **A:** 43, 44
Singer, Isaac
    **A:** 30, 32 (ill.)
Singer Manufacturing Company
    **A:** 30, 32
Sioux
    **B:** 183
**Sitting Bull**
    **A:** 108, 109
    **B:** 183 (ill.), **183–91,** 190 (ill.)
    **PS:** 13–20, 17 (ill.)
    battles U.S. troops, **B:** 184–86
    Creelman interview, **PS:** 14–17
    death of, **B:** 187–91
    early years, **B:** 183–84
    exile and surrender, **B:** 186–87
    Plains Indian Wars, **PS:** 14
Sixteenth Amendment
    **A:** 271
Skyscrapers
    **A:** 96–97, 218
Slaughterhouses. *See* Meatpacking industry
Slaves, emancipation of
    **PS:** 87, 97
SLP (Socialist Labor Party)
    **A:** 57
Slums
    **PS:** 62–63, 70
Smoking
    **PS:** 132–33, 134, 206
Smuggling
    **A:** 81
    **PS:** 10
Social classes
    **A:** 95, 131, 135, 171–74, 216
    **B:** 54, 56, 175
    fashion among, **PS:** 122
    Gibson, Charles Dana, on, **PS:** 109–11
    in Gilded Age and Progressive Era, **PS:** 211–12
    industrialization, **PS:** 53, 61–62, 163

Riis, Jacob, on, *PS:* 68–69
on *Titanic, PS:* 212, 214–15,
221–22, 224–25
Social Darwinism
*A:* 31, 171, 176
*PS:* 53
Social Democratic Party
*A:* 58
Social Gospel movement
*A:* 219
*PS:* 54
Socialism
*A:* 57, 58, 59, 61, 278
*B:* 112, 175–76, 177, 181
*PS:* 199
Socialist Labor Party (SLP)
*A:* 57
Socialist Party of America
*A:* 57, 58
Society for the Improvement
and Colonization of East
European Jews
*PS:* 24
Society of Friends. *See* Quakers
Sodus Bay & Southern Railroad
*B:* 76
Sojourners
*A:* 66, 67, 80, 88–89, 93
*PS:* 1
Soldiers
*B:* 128, 154–55
*PS:* 167
Soldiers, Buffalo. *See* Buffalo
Soldiers
*Solitude of Self* (Stanton)
*B:* 207
**Solomon, Hannah**
*B:* 193 (ill.), **193–201**
Chicago Woman's Club,
*B:* 194–95
early years, *B:* 193–94
legacy, *B:* 199–200
National Council of Jewish
Women, *B:* 196–98
Solomon, Henry
*B:* 195

Sommer, Frank
*PS:* 200
*The Son of the Wolf* (London)
*B:* 114
*The Souls of Black Folk* (Du Bois)
*A:* 212–13
South Dakota
*B:* 90
South Improvement Company
*A:* 32
*PS:* 153–54, 155–58
Southern Farmers' Alliance
*A:* 141
Southern Pacific Railroad
*B:* 80
Southern states
*PS:* 87
Democratic Party, *A:* 3
economy, *A:* 1, 21
immigrants, *A:* 72
Reconstruction Era, *A:* 1–3
Southwestern states
*PS:* 140, 144
Spain
*A:* 161, 167
*B:* 23, 63, 129–30, 153–55
Spanish-American War
*A:* 19, 167, 257–58
*B:* 128, 129–30, 153–55, 216
Spanish Civil War
*B:* 63
Speaker, Tris
*B:* 30, 31
Speech, freedom of
*B:* 60
Spencer, Herbert
*A:* 31
*PS:* 53
Spending, government
*B:* 91
Spoils system. *See* Patronage
Sports
*A:* 219–25
Square deal
*B:* 158
Stalwarts
*A:* 13, 14, 16

Stampeders
*A:* 234–37, 237 (ill.), 238,
239–40
Standard Oil Company
*B:* 100, 163
big business, *A:* 26–27
creation of, *A:* 32
dismantling of, *A:* 36–37
industrialization, *A:* 23–24
monopoly, *A:* 33 (ill.), 33–34
Rockefeller, John D.,
*PS:* 152–59
Sears Modern Homes,
*PS:* 193–94
Tarbell, Ida, on, *A:* 35–36, 207
**Stanton, Elizabeth Cady**
*A:* 182
*B:* 203 (ill.), **203–10**
*PS:* 74, 76, 78, 80
activist beginnings, *B:* 204–5
Anthony, Susan B., *B:* 203,
206 (ill.), 206–7
early years, *B:* 203–4
Gage, Matilda Joslyn,
*B:* 208, 209
Seneca Falls Convention,
*B:* 205–6
women's suffrage, *B:* 206–8
Stanton, Henry B.
*B:* 204
Stark, John Stilwell
*B:* 106
Starr, Belle
*A:* 118, 118 (ill.)
Starr, Ellen Gates
*A:* 186
*B:* 3, 3 (ill.), 4, 7
Starr, Sam
*A:* 118
Statue of Liberty
*A:* 69
*B:* 17
*PS:* 21–22, 22 (ill.), 23,
25, 27
Steamships
*B:* 222–24

Steel industry
  *A:* 26, 54–56
  *B:* 57–59
  *PS:* 52
Steelworkers Union. *See*
  Amalgamated Association of
  Iron, Steel and Tin Workers
Steffens, Lincoln
  *A:* 186, 260
  *B:* 100, 156
Stephens, Uriah S.
  *A:* 48
Stereotypes
  *A:* 79, 85
  *PS:* 34
Sterilization
  *A:* 176
Stetson, Charles Walter
  *B:* 178, 179
Stieglitz, Alfred
  *A:* 217–18
Stilwell, Mary
  *B:* 45
*The Sting* (motion picture)
  *B:* 107
Stock market crashes
  *A:* 32–33
Stocks, watered
  *B:* 225
Stockyards. *See also* Meatpacking
  industry
  *PS:* 164, 165
Stoewer, Willy
  *PS:* 222 (ill.)
Stokes, Lottie
  *B:* 109
Stone, Amasa
  *PS:* 157
Stone, Lucy
  *PS:* 74
"Story of a Great Monopoly"
  (Lloyd)
  *A:* 33
"The Story of a Susceptible
  Bachelor" (artwork)
  *PS:* 115 (ill.)

Stowe, Harriet Beecher
  *A:* 103
  *B:* 178
Streetcars
  *A:* 95
Streeter, Alson J.
  *A:* 10, 135
Strentzel, Louise Wanda (Louie)
  *B:* 135
Strikes. *See* Labor movement
Stryker, Roy
  *B:* 102–3
"Studies in Expression—When
  Women Are Jurors" (artwork)
  *PS:* 114 (ill.)
*Studies in Logical Theory*
  *B:* 37
"Studies in the Sierras" (Muir)
  *B:* 135
Subsidies
  *A:* 137
Suburbs
  *A:* 95–96, 97
Subways
  *A:* 220
Suffrage, African American
  *PS:* 74, 97, 98
Suffrage, women's. *See* Women's
  suffrage movement
Sullivan, John
  *A:* 222
Sullivan, Louis
  *A:* 218
Sundance Kid
  *A:* 118
Supplies
  *A:* 238
Supreme Court, U.S.
  *A:* 12
  *Brown v. Board of Education,*
    *PS:* 103
  *Plessy v. Ferguson, PS:* 98,
    100–102
Susan B. Anthony Amendment.
  *See* Nineteenth Amendment
Sustainable agriculture
  *A:* 120–21

Sweatshops
  *A:* 53, 190–91
  *PS:* 198
Swift & Company
  *A:* 260
  *B:* 157
  *PS:* 165, 169 (ill.)
Swift, Gustavus
  *PS:* 165, 165 (ill.)

**T**

Taft-Katsura Agreement
  *A:* 268
  *B:* 167
Taft, Nellie
  *A:* 275
Taft, William Howard
  *B:* 168, 169, 170
  conservation movement, *A:* 124
  immigration policy, *A:* 82
  presidency overview,
    *A:* 270–76, 271 (ill.),
    273 (ill.)
  presidential election of 1912,
    *A:* 275–77, 277 (ill.)
Tall tales
  *A:* 120
Tammany Hall
  *A:* 4, 76, 151
  *B:* 144
Tarbell, Ida M.
  *A:* 35–36, 36 (ill.), 186, 207,
    259–60
  *B:* 100, 156
  *PS:* 151–61, 154 (ill.)
Tariff Act of 1883
  *A:* 16
  *B:* 15
Tariffs. *See also* McKinley Tariff
  of 1890
  *B:* 84, 90, 122, 126–27
  Cleveland, Grover, *A:* 17, 18
  gold standard vs., *A:* 143, 145
  McKinley, William,
    *A:* 136–38, 163–64

political aspects, *A:* 6–7
Taft, William Howard,
   *A:* 271, 272
Tatanka Iyotanka. *See* Sitting Bull
Taxes and taxation
   *A:* 6–7, 164
   *B:* 126–27
   *PS:* 57
Technology
   *A:* 22, 204
Tecumseh
   *A:* 100
   *PS:* 32
Teddy bears
   *B:* 160, 160 (ill.)
Telegraphs
   *A:* 21, 22, 248–49
   *B:* 44–47
Telephones
   *A:* 248–50
Temperance League
   *B:* 248 (ill.)
Temperance movement
   *A:* 145, 181
   *B:* 204, 245, 246–50,
     248 (ill.)
   *PS:* 75–76
Tenancy. *See also* Agriculture
   *A:* 132
Tenement House Act of 1901
   *A:* 185
   *PS:* 70
Tenement House Commission
   *B:* 101
Tenements
   *A:* 23, 24 (ill.), 74, 84 (ill.),
     84–85, 87, 183–85, 184 (ill.)
   *PS:* 68 (ill.), 69 (ill.), 70, 71
Tennessee
   *B:* 123
Tennessee Valley Authority
   (TVA)
   *B:* 101
Tenure of Office Act
   *A:* 153
   *B:* 15–16, 17

Territorial expansion
   Cleveland, Grover,
     *B:* 19, 22–23
   Harrison, Benjamin, *B:* 89–90
   McKinley, William, *B:* 128–29
   Roosevelt, Theodore,
     *B:* 164–65
   Twain, Mark, *B:* 216
Test-tube babies
   *A:* 254
Texas & Pacific Railroad
   *B:* 71
Texas Medley Quartette
   *B:* 106
Thaw, Harry Kendall
   *PS:* 111
Thirteenth Amendment
   *PS:* 97, 98
Thomas A. Edison, Incorporated
   *B:* 50
Thompson-Houston
   *B:* 48
Thompson, J. Edgar
   *PS:* 156
Thoreau, Henry David
   *A:* 120
"Thought and Its Subject-Matter"
   (Dewey)
   *B:* 37
Tilden, Samuel
   *A:* 6, 10
*Titanic* (motion picture)
   *PS:* 224–25, 225 (ill.)
*Titanic* (ship)
   *PS:* 213 (ill.), 215 (ill.),
     217 (ill.), 222 (ill.)
   "Dr. Dodge's Wife Tells
     Story of *Titanic* Wreck,"
     *PS:* 214–20
   history, *PS:* 212, 214
   salvage operations, *PS:* 224–25
Tobacco industry
   *B:* 32–33, 33 (ill.)
   *PS:* 126, 128 (ill.)
Tobin, Margaret. *See* Brown,
   Margaret Tobin (Unsinkable
   Molly Brown)

Topps
   *B:* 33
Torlino, Tom
   *PS:* 33 (ill.)
Toynbee Hall (London, England)
   *B:* 3
Trade, international.
   *See* International trade
Trading cards, baseball.
   *See* Baseball cards
Transmitters
   *B:* 46–47
Trans-Siberian Railroad
   *B:* 166–67
Travel journals
   *A:* 119
Treaty of Fort Wayne
   *PS:* 32
Treaty of Greenville
   *A:* 100
   *PS:* 31, 32
Treaty of Portsmouth
   *B:* 167
*Treemonisha* (Joplin)
   *B:* 108–9
Triangle Shirtwaist Company fire
   *A:* 85, 190 (ill.), 190–91
   *PS:* 197–209, 201 (ill.),
     205 (ill.), 206 (ill.)
   *Chicago Sunday Tribune* article,
     *PS:* 202–4
   impact of, *PS:* 204–7
   working conditions,
     *PS:* 197–200
Trolleys
   *A:* 95
Trusts and trustbusting. *See also*
   Antitrust actions
   *A:* 27, 33, 34–35, 158, 164–65
   *B:* 80, 127, 156
   *PS:* 152, 153
Truth-in-advertising movement
   *A:* 205
Turner, Frederick Jackson
   *A:* 112, 112 (ill.)
Tuskegee Institute
   *A:* 195–96

***B:*** 229, 230–33, 231 (ill.)
***PS:*** 99
TVA (Tennessee Valley Authority)
***B:*** 101
**Twain, Mark**
  ***A:*** 120, 149, 199, 209–10
  ***B:*** 211 (ill.), **211–20,**
    215 (ill.), 218 (ill.)
  ***PS:*** 4, 4 (ill.)
  anti-imperialism, ***B:*** 128
  Chautauqua movement,
    ***B:*** 216, 217
  early years, ***B:*** 212–13
  John Chinaman, ***B:*** 147
  later years, ***B:*** 216–19
  popularity of, ***B:*** 211, 217, 219
  sayings, ***B:*** 216
  writing career, ***B:*** 213–15
Tweed, William Marcy "Boss"
  ***A:*** 4 (ill.), 4–5, 76, 206–7, 211
    (ill.)
  ***B:*** 67–68, 143–45, 145 (ill.),
    146 (ill.)
Twenty-second Amendment
  ***A:*** 14

## U

UK (United Kingdom). *See* Great
  Britain
UMWA (United Mine Workers
  of America)
  ***A:*** 60, 62
Uncle Jumbo. *See* Cleveland, Grover
Uncle Sam
  ***PS:*** 120 (ill.)
"Uncle Sam's Idea"/ Wabash
  (Sears Modern Home Numbers
  248 and 2003)
  ***PS:*** 186 (ill.)
*Uncle Tom's Cabin* (Stowe)
  ***A:*** 103
Unconscious mind
  ***A:*** 254
Unger, William
  ***B:*** 45

Union Labor Party (ULP)
  ***A:*** 10, 135
Union Pacific Railroad
  ***A:*** 121
  ***B:*** 70, 77, 80
Union Stock Yards
  ***PS:*** 166, 173
Unions, labor. *See* Labor
  movement
Unitarianism
  ***A:*** 273
United Hebrew Trades
  ***A:*** 85–86
United Kingdom (UK). *See* Great
  Britain
United Labor Party
  ***A:*** 10
United Mine Workers of America
  (UMWA)
  ***A:*** 60, 62
University of Chicago
  ***B:*** 37, 39
University of Illinois at Chicago
  ***B:*** 7
Unsinkable Molly Brown. *See*
  Brown, Margaret Tobin
  (Unsinkable Molly Brown)
*Up from Slavery* (Washington)
  ***B:*** 229, 234
Upper Deck
  ***B:*** 33
Uprising of the 20,000 (strike)
  ***PS:*** 199
Upton, Harriet Taylor
  ***PS:*** 81 (ill.)
Urban areas
  ***A:*** 23, 93–98, 182–85, 217
U.S. Bureau of Indian Affairs (BIA)
  ***A:*** 104
U.S. Bureau of the Census
  ***A:*** 110–11
U.S. Children's Bureau
  ***B:*** 5
U.S. Civil Service Commission
  ***B:*** 14, 153
U.S. Congress

American Antiquities Act,
  ***PS:*** 139–48
Chinese Exclusion Act,
  ***PS:*** 1–11
Dawes Severalty Act,
  ***PS:*** 31–39
U.S. Department of Agriculture
  ***A:*** 123
  ***B:*** 164
  ***PS:*** 172
U.S. Department of Commerce
  and Labor
  ***B:*** 158
U.S. Department of Labor
  ***B:*** 123
U.S. Department of the Interior
  ***B:*** 164
  ***PS:*** 142
U.S. Division of Forestry
  ***B:*** 164
U.S. Food and Drug Administration
  ***PS:*** 171
U.S. Forest Service
  ***B:*** 164
U.S. Navy
  ***B:*** 87
U.S. Pension Bureau
  ***B:*** 17–18
U.S. Steel
  ***A:*** 35, 272
  ***PS:*** 52
U.S. Supreme Court
  ***A:*** 12
  *Brown v. Board of Education,*
    ***PS:*** 103
  *Plessy v. Ferguson,* ***PS:*** 98,
    100–102

## V

Vandalism
  ***PS:*** 143, 144
**Vanderbilt, Cornelius**
  ***A:*** 26, 27, 27 (ill.)
  ***B:*** 221 (ill.), **221–28**
  ***PS:*** 52, 156

early years, **B:** 221–22
Gould, Jay, **B:** 67–69
legacy of wealth,
  **B:** 227–28
philanthropy, **B:** 226–27
railroads, **B:** 224–26, 226 (ill.)
steamship industry, **B:** 222–24
Vanderbilt, Cornelius II
  **B:** 227
Vanderbilt family
  **B:** 227
Vanderbilt, Frederick William
  **B:** 228
Vanderbilt, Gloria
  **B:** 227
*Vanderbilt* (ship)
  **B:** 224
Vanderbilt, Sophia
  **B:** 227, 228
Vanderbilt, William Henry
  **B:** 227
Vanzetti, Bartolomeo
  **A:** 213
  **B:** 181
Vaudeville
  **A:** 226, 227
Venezuela
  **A:** 161, 262
  **B:** 22–23, 158
Vertical integration
  **A:** 26, 30
  **PS:** 165
Veterans
  **A:** 17, 153–54
  **B:** 17–18
Veto power
  **A:** 17, 153–54
  **B:** 16
Victorianism
  **A:** 177
Victrola
  **A:** 229
Vincent, John H.
  **B:** 217
Violence, labor. *See* Labor
  violence

Violence, racial. *See* Racial
  violence
Vitascope
  **B:** 50
Voting rights
  African Americans,
    **PS:** 74, 97, 98
  women, **PS:** 73–75

## W

Wabash Railroad
  **B:** 71
Wabash/"Uncle Sam's Idea"
  (Sears Modern Home Numbers
  248 and 2003)
  **PS:** 186 (ill.)
Wages
  coal mining, **A:** 40, 41–42,
    44; **PS:** 135
  garment industry, **PS:** 70,
    198–99
  meatpacking, **PS:** 166
  steel industry, **A:** 54
Wagner, Sally Roesch
  **B:** 188–91
Wald, Lillian
  **B:** 4 (ill.), 4–5
Ward, Aaron Montgomery
  **A:** 208
Warfare, guerrilla
  **B:** 130
Warner, Charles Dudley
  **A:** 149, 199, 209–10
  **B:** 214
**Washington, Booker T.**
  **A:** 195–96, 196 (ill.), 275
  **B:** 229 (ill.), **229–35**
  **PS:** 85, 99, 99 (ill.), 100
  early years, **B:** 229–30
  leadership role,
    **B:** 233–34
  Roosevelt, Theodore, **B:** 159,
    234, 234 (ill.)
  Tuskegee Institute, **B:** 229,
    230–33

Washington (state)
  **PS:** 38
Water conservation
  **A:** 124
Watered stocks
  **B:** 225
Watson, Peter H.
  **PS:** 155, 156
Watson, Thomas
  **A:** 248, 249, 249 (ill.)
WBA (Workers Benevolent
  Association)
  **A:** 43, 45–47
WCTU (Woman's Christian
  Temperance Union)
  **A:** 145
  **B:** 245, 246, 247, 248, 249–50
  **PS:** 76, 81
"The Weaker Sex" (artwork)
  **PS:** 114 (ill.)
Wealth
  **B:** 170, 227–28
*Wealth against Commonwealth*
  (Lloyd)
  **A:** 33
Wealth distribution
  **A:** 23, 135–36, 149, 171, 173
  **PS:** 53, 54–56, 211–12
Wealth, Gospel of. *See* "The
  Gospel of Wealth"
Weaver, James B.
  **A:** 9, 15, 142
*Weekly Bazaar* (publication)
  **PS:** 108
Weeks Act of 1911
  **A:** 124
Weeks, John W.
  **A:** 124
Weldon, Catherine
  **B:** 188, 189
Welfare. *See* Government assistance
Wells, Ida B. *See* Wells-Barnett,
  Ida B.
**Wells-Barnett, Ida B.**
  **A:** 140–41, 141 (ill.)
  **B:** 237 (ill.), **237–44**
  **PS:** 83–95, 86 (ill.)

activism, *B:* 238

anti-lynching crusade, *B:* 239, 241–42, 243

at Columbian Exposition, *PS:* 85–87

early years, *B:* 237–38

journalism career, *B:* 238–39, 241

later years, *B:* 242–43

National Association for the Advancement of Colored People, *B:* 242

"The Reason Why the Colored American Is Not in the World's Columbian Exposition," *PS:* 87–92

Wells Fargo Express Company *B:* 81

West, American. *See* American West; Westward expansion

Western Union Telegraph Company *B:* 44, 45, 70

Westinghouse Electric Company *B:* 163

Westward expansion

conservation movement, *A:* 120–24

literature, *A:* 118–21

Native American impact, *A:* 99–105, 108–11

outlaws, *A:* 116–18

railroad industry, *A:* 111, 113–16

*A Wheel within a Wheel* (Willard) *B:* 249

Wheeler-Howard Act of 1934. *See* Indian Reorganization Act of 1934

Whig Party *A:* 14

*White Fang* (London) *B:* 115

White Pass *A:* 236–37

White, Stanford *PS:* 110, 111

White supremacy. *See also* Ku Klux Klan (KKK) *A:* 3, 140 *B:* 239

Wiley, Harvey *A:* 264 *B:* 162

**Willard, Frances** *A:* 145 *B:* 245 (ill.), **245–51**, 247 (ill.) *PS:* 73–82, 77 (ill.)

early years, *B:* 245–46

legacy, *B:* 249–50

National Council of Women of the United States speech, *PS:* 77–80

temperance movement, *B:* 246–47, 249; *PS:* 76

women's movement, *PS:* 76–80

Willis, Elizabeth *B:* 181

Wilson, Woodrow *B:* 62, 123, 170, 181 *PS:* 57, 80, 81 (ill.), 142, 146

antitrust actions, *A:* 34–35

immigration policy, *A:* 82

presidency overview, *A:* 276–79, 279 (ill.)

presidential election of 1912, *A:* 276

Winslet, Kate *PS:* 224, 225 (ill.)

Wire, barbed. *See* Barbed wire

Witt, Stillman *PS:* 157

Wizard of Menlo Park. *See* Edison, Thomas

*The Wizard of Oz* (Baum) *B:* 209

*The Wizard of Oz* (motion picture) *A:* 146 (ill.), 146–47

Wizards of the Coast *B:* 33

WNLU (Woman's National Liberal Union) *B:* 209

Wobblies. *See* Industrial Workers of the World (IWW)

*Woman Rebel* (publication) *A:* 174

*Woman Suffrage and Politics: The Inner Story of the Suffrage Movement* (Catt) *PS:* 75

*The Woman's Bible* (Stanton) *B:* 207 *PS:* 80

Woman's Christian Temperance Union (WCTU) *B:* 245, 246, 247, 248, 249–50 *PS:* 76, 81

"Woman's Holy War" (Currier and Ives) *B:* 248 (ill.)

Woman's National Liberal Union (WNLU), *B:* 209

Women. *See also* Feminism; Women's suffrage movement; Working women

activists in Chicago, *B:* 200

Addams, Jane, 1–9

African American, *A:* 180

automobiles, *A:* 224–25

Chinese, *A:* 79, 80

Cleveland, Grover, *A:* 157; *B:* 20

conservation movement, *A:* 123

frontier, *PS:* 41–42

Gibson Girl, *PS:* 108–11, 112 (ill.), 113 (ill.), 114 (ill.), 115 (ill.), 116 (ill.), 117 (ill.), 118 (ill.), 119 (ill.), 120–22

Gilded Age, *A:* 25

Gilman, Charlotte Perkins, *B:* 178–79

Goldman, Emma, 53–64

gold prospectors, *A:* 241

Hine, Lewis, *B:* 101

outlaws, *A:* 118

Progressive Era, *A:* 174–75, 177–82

Progressive Party, **B:** 170
Roosevelt, Theodore, **B:** 168
social reform, **B:** 194–95
Solomon, Hannah, **B:** 193–201
Stanton, Elizabeth Cady,
 **B:** 203–10
Taft, William Howard,
 **A:** 274–75
temperance movement, **A:** 145
Washington, Booker T., **B:** 234
Wells-Barnett, Ida B., 237–44
Western, **A:** 119
Willard, Frances, **B:** 245–51
Wilson, Woodrow, **A:** 278
*Women and Economics* (Gilman)
 **B:** 179
Women's International League
 for Peace and Freedom
 **B:** 8
Women's National Indian
 Association
 **A:** 102
Women's Peace Party
 **B:** 8
Women's rights movement
 **PS:** 73–74, 76–80
Women's suffrage movement. *See
 also* Nineteenth Amendment
 **A:** 179–82, 181 (ill.), 278
 **PS:** 73–75, 77
 Addams, Jane, **B:** 7
 Anthony, Susan B., **B:** 203,
 206–7
 Bryan, William Jennings,
 **B:** 122
 Cleveland, Grover, **B:** 20
 Gage, Matilda Joslyn, **B:** 206,
 207, 208–9
 Goldman, Emma, **B:** 60
 resistance to, **B:** 205
 Roosevelt, Theodore, **B:** 169
 Solomon, Hannah,
 **B:** 198–99
 Stanton, Elizabeth Cady,
 **B:** 203, 206–8
 temperance movement,
 **B:** 247, 249–50

Wells-Barnett, Ida B.,
 **B:** 242–43
Willard, Frances,
 **B:** 245
Women's Trade Union League
 (WTUL)
 **A:** 179
 **PS:** 199
Wood, Joe
 **B:** 31
Wood, Leonard
 **B:** 154
Workers Benevolent Association
 (WBA)
 **A:** 43, 45–47
Working conditions
 garment industry, **PS:** 197,
 198, 200
 Sinclair, Upton, on, **PS:** 164,
 166–71
Working women
 **A:** 25
 **B:** 101
 **PS:** 200–201
Works Project Administration
 (WPA)
 **B:** 103
World War I
 **A:** 278
 **B:** 61–62
World's Anti-Slavery Convention
 of 1904
 **B:** 204
World's Columbian Exposition.
 *See* Columbian Exposition
Wounded Knee Massacre
 **A:** 109–11, 111 (ill.)
 **PS:** 18, 47
Wovoka
 **A:** 108
WPA (Works Project
 Administration)
 **B:** 103
Wright, Frank Lloyd
 **A:** 218
Wright, Orville
 **A:** 241–47, 246 (ill.), 248

Wright, Wilbur
 **A:** 241–47, 248, 248 (ill.)
WTUL (Women's Trade Union
 League)
 **A:** 179
Wyoming
 **B:** 90

Xenophobia
 **A:** 82

**Y**

"The Yellow Wallpaper"
 (Gilman)
 **B:** 179
Yellowstone National Park
 **A:** 121
Yellowstone National Park
 Protection Act of 1894
 **PS:** 140
YMCA (Young Men's Christian
 Association)
 **B:** 242
Yosemite
 **B:** 133, 134, 135, 136
"Yosemite Glaciers" (Muir)
 **B:** 135
Young, Ella Flagg
 **B:** 94, 200
Young Men's Christian
 Association (YMCA)
 **B:** 242
Yukon
 **A:** 233–37, 239–41
Yukon Gold Rush
 **B:** 114

**Z**

Zoning
 **A:** 183